NON-MARKET SOCIALISM IN THE NINETEENTH AND TWENTIETH CENTURIES

Also by Maximilien Rubel

PAGES DE KARL MARX POUR UNE ÉTHIQUE SOCIALISTE
KARL MARX: SELECTED WRITINGS IN SOCIOLOGY AND SOCIAL PHILOSOPHY (*editor with T.B. Bottomore*)
KARL MARX: OEUVRES: ÉCONOMIE I, II
PHILOSOPHIE (*editor*)
KARL MARX UND FRIEDRICH ENGELS ZUR RUSSISCHEN REVOLUTION: Kritik Eines Mythos
MARX WITHOUT MYTH (*with Margaret Manale*)
RUBEL ON KARL MARX: Five Essays

Also by John Crump

THE ORIGINS OF SOCIALIST THOUGHT IN JAPAN
STATE CAPITALISM: The Wages System under New Management (*with Adam Buick*)

Non-Market Socialism in the Nineteenth and Twentieth Centuries

Edited by
Maximilien Rubel
and
John Crump

St. Martin's Press New York

First published in the United States of America in 1987

Printed in Hong Kong

ISBN 0–312–00524–5

Library of Congress Cataloging-in-Publication Data
Non-market socialism.

Edited papers from a conference held in
York, England, Sept. 1984.
Bibliography: p.
Includes index.
1. Socialism — Congresses. 2. Communism—
Congresses. 3. Marxian economics—Congresses.
4. Anarchism—Congresses. I. Rubel, Maximilien.
II. Crump, John 1944– .
HX13.A3N66 1987 335 86–29847
ISBN 0–312–00524–5

This book is dedicated to the men and women of the thin red line of non-market socialism who have kept alive the vision of socialism as a society of personal freedom, communal solidarity, production for use and free access to goods.

Contents

Notes on the Contributors

Maximilien Rubel retired from the Centre national de la recherche scientifique in 1970 as Maître de recherche honoraire and joined the Institut de sciences mathématiques et économiques appliquées in 1959 as the editor of *Etudes de Marxologie*. He was born in Czernowitz (then in Austro-Hungary, now in Russia) in 1905 and has lived in France since 1931. His numerous books and articles include *Pages de Karl Marx pour une éthique socialiste*; *Karl Marx: Selected Writings in Sociology and Social Philosophy* (with T. B. Bottomore); *Karl Marx, Oeuvres: Economie* I, *Economie* II, *Philosophie*; *Karl Marx und Friedrich Engels zur russischen Revolution: Kritik eines Mythos*; *Marx Without Myth* (with Margaret Manale); *Rubel on Karl Marx: Five Essays.*

Adam Buick is a civil servant with the Commission of European Communities in Luxemburg. He was formerly head of the National Union of Mineworkers' social insurance department. He is the author (with John Crump) of *State Capitalism: the Wages System under New Management.*

Stephen Coleman is a Lecturer in the History of Ideas at the London campus of an American university. He received his Ph D from the University of London in 1984 for a thesis on *The Origin and Meaning of the Political Theory of Impossibilism.*

John Crump is a Lecturer in Politics at the University of York and the author of *The Origins of Socialist Thought in Japan* and (with Adam Buick) *State Capitalism: the Wages System under New Management.*

Alain Pengam works as a proof-reader in Paris.

Mark Shipway, after studying politics at the University of York, began research into the anti-parliamentary communist movement in Britain between the two world wars, for which he was awarded a Ph D by the University of Manchester in 1985.

Preface

This book is the result of a collaborative effort by a group of people who, as individuals, have their differences, particularly over the question of how socialism might be brought about. What has united us and given impetus to our joint venture has been our common commitment to a vision of socialism which we attempt to convey in this book. All of us are fired by a passion for socialism, which we see as the only hope for a world which capitalism is propelling towards catastrophe.

Although each of us takes responsibility for the chapter that bears our name, we have made considerable efforts to produce a book which focuses on a common theme and employs a consistent terminology. In order to achieve this, we gathered in York in September 1984 for a strenuous weekend of debate and forthright criticism of each other's work, which at that stage existed only in draft form. We were assisted in this process by a number of people who, while not contributing chapters of their own, gave generously of their time in order to join our discussions. These were: Amanda Burls, Adrian Leftwich, Theresa McCoy, Nigel Morgan and Michael Ridge. We wish to express our gratitude to them and to make it clear that none of them is responsible for the conclusions reached in this book. Thanks are also due to Midorikawa Taeko, who kept us fed over the weekend.

Following the York conference, we dispersed and wrote the final versions of our respective chapters. These chapters have since been edited with an eye to technical detail and literary style, but no attempt has been made to impose a common political line. Consequently, astute readers will notice differences of emphasis and nuance between the various contributions. Such readers will be struck even more forcefully, however, by the way in which each contributor, from his particular angle, conveys the core ideas of non-market socialism.

Introduction

The theme of this book is 'non-market socialism'. This term demands an explanation at an early stage of the book. We are well aware that 'non-market socialism' is – to use the current jargon – a pleonasm. In other words, if we use words accurately, it is unnecessary to qualify 'socialism' with 'non-market' because socialism is, by definition, a marketless society. The market cannot coexist with socialism because socialism means that society owns and controls both the means of production and the goods which result from productive activity. For the market to exist, some sectional interest (an individual, a joint-stock company, a nationalised concern, a workers' cooperative and so on) has to be in control of part of the social product, which it then disposes of by entering into exchange relations with others. Exchange cannot take place when society, and none other, controls the means of production and the social product. Far from socialism being compatible with exchange and the market, the generalised production of goods for exchange on the market is the hallmark of an entirely different type of society – capitalism.

If socialism means the social ownership of the means of production and the fruits of production, so too does communism. The terms 'socialism' and 'communism' are used interchangeably in this book because, just as there is no distinction between *society* and the *community*, so *social* ownership and *communal* ownership are equally indistinguishable. Contrary to Lenin's assertions, socialism is not a partial and incomplete first stage of communism.

Yet though it is a simple matter logically to define socialism/communism, it is politics and not logic which determines how words are (mis)used within capitalism. Dispensing with logic, those who wield political power in all parts of the world have an interest in misrepresenting socialism. Thanks to their unrelenting efforts, the word 'socialism' has taken on the spurious meaning of state enterprises employing wage-earners in order to produce goods for sale on the market. In Chapter 2, John Crump demonstrates how both Social Democracy and Leninism have played an important role in bringing about the popular identification of 'socialism' with state capitalism.

It is in the face of this situation that we have chosen to use the term 'non-market socialism'. Our purpose is straightforward, and we do not hide it. We want to re-establish the genuine meaning of socialism. We are not arguing that absence of the market is the sole defining feature of socialism. On the contrary, socialism is not merely a marketless society; it is also a stateless society, a classless society, a moneyless society, a wageless society . . . and so on. However, in choosing to use the term 'non-market socialism', we are selecting one among a number of qualities which socialism possesses (its characteristic of being a marketless society) and focusing on this in order to stress the difference between socialism and all varieties of capitalism.

Undoubtedly, our use of the term 'non-market socialism' is not without danger. Maximilien Rubel brings out this point in Chapter 1. By talking in terms of 'non-market socialism', we may inadvertently imply that other varieties of socialism (even '*market* socialism'!) could exist. Nothing could be further from our intention, of course. But at least 'non-market socialism' does have the merit of emphasising firstly that the marketless society of socialism has never been established anywhere in the world, and secondly that most so-called 'socialists' are nothing of the sort. The fact that Social Democrats, Leninists and other supposed 'socialists' or 'communists' envisage a role for the market, tells us that they represent forces for maintaining capitalism, not for achieving socialism.

One final point needs to be made with regard to our terminology. Despite the inaccuracy of calling an organisation such as the Communist Party of Great Britain (CPGB) a communist party, or the Socialist Party of Italy (PSI) a socialist party, we have regarded organisational labels simply as proper names which deserve to be used neutrally. Hence our references to organisations such as the CPGB and PSI do not imply any recognition of their supposedly 'communist' or 'socialist' (in fact, state capitalist) character.

In Chapter 1, Maximilien Rubel looks at 'Non-Market Socialism in the Nineteenth Century'. Rubel explains that rejection of the market was an integral component of Marx's and Engels's conception of socialism and he demonstrates that the approach which Marx and Engels adopted towards this question separated them from Proudhon and the other false 'socialists' of their day. Rubel's chapter is complemented by Alain Pengam's discussion in Chapter 3 of other nineteenth-century, non-market socialists, such as Joseph Déjacque and Peter Kropotkin.

In Chapter 2, John Crump examines 'Non-Market Socialism in the Twentieth Century'. In addition to identifying those currents which have represented the 'thin red line' of non-market socialism in the twentieth century, Crump identifies a number of key principles which distinguish non-market socialists from Social Democrats, Leninists and other advocates of capitalism. These key principles have served as litmus paper, as it were, in deciding which currents to include in a book on non-market socialism and which to exclude.

The currents which have adhered to these principles are presented in roughly the order of their historical appearance in Chapters 3 to 7. In Chapter 3, Alain Pengam differentiates 'Anarcho-Communism' from other varieties of anarchism. In Chapter 4, Stephen Coleman discusses 'Impossibilism' in general and the Socialist Party of Great Britain in particular. In Chapter 5, Mark Shipway examines 'Council Communism', paying particular attention to the theories of Anton Pannekoek. Similarly, in Chapter 6 on 'Bordigism', Adam Buick focuses principally on the ideas of Amadeo Bordiga. Finally, in Chapter 7 on 'Situationism', Mark Shipway analyses the ideas of the situationists. Some of the writers identify more closely with the currents about which they have written than others, but all were given the brief of producing chapters which fulfilled three objectives. First, each chapter provides a brief historical account of the current under examination. Second, each chapter outlines the principal theoretical ideas of the current. Third, each writer gives a personal assessment of the strengths and weaknesses of the current.

It may be useful for readers to have an overall picture of the various currents which have represented non-market socialism in the twentieth century before they tackle the detailed, chapter-by-chapter analyses of each current. Accordingly, we present brief profiles of these five currents here.

ANARCHO-COMMUNISM

Anarcho-communism's roots extend back to the activity and writings in the nineteenth century of anarchists such as Peter Kropotkin, Elisée Reclus and Jean Grave. One of anarcho-communism's fullest expositions in this century was Alexander Berkman's *What Is Communist Anarchism?* (1929), better known in its abridged form as the *ABC of Anarchism* (1942). As examples of anarcho-communist revolutionary activity, we could point to the struggles of the Partido Liberal Mexicano in the Mexican Revolution and to some anarchist groups in the Russian Revolution. In both these revolutions, anarcho-communists worked with peasants and workers, encouraged them to substitute their own organisations for those of the state, and participated in attempts to organise production on the basis of free communes. What distinguishes anarcho-communism from other varieties of anarchism is the equal emphasis which anarcho-communism has placed on individual freedom and communal solidarity, and its belief that these twin goals can be achieved simultaneously through the establishment of a stateless, moneyless communist society.

IMPOSSIBILISM

'Possibilism' and 'impossibilism' were terms coined in the nineteenth century to distinguish different wings of the Social Democratic Parties. Social Democrats who concentrated their efforts on reforming capitalism were dubbed 'possibilists', while the 'impossibilists' were those who struggled solely to achieve the goal of socialism. In time, the impossibilists either split away from the Social Democratic Parties, or abandoned impossibilism as the price for remaining in the ranks of Social Democracy. In Britain, impossibilism has its roots in various revolts against the leadership of the first Social Democratic organisation to be formed, the Social Democratic Federation of 1884. Secessions from the Social Democratic Federation led to the formation, as early as 1884, of the Socialist League, in which William Morris was a prominent participant, and to the emergence in 1904 of the Socialist Party of Great Britain (SPGB). The SPGB has become the best-known impossibilist group, and its journal, the *Socialist Standard*, is the most accessible written expression of impossibilism.

COUNCIL COMMUNISM

Although both workers' councils and groups which later formed the nuclei of the council communist movement existed before the First World War, council communism rose to brief prominence, principally in Germany, immediately following the War. Inspired by the Russian Revolution, the council communists saw the workers' councils (soviets) as the instrument of proletarian revolution. In a number of West European countries, groups of council communists were constituent elements in the Communist Parties when these were first formed, but they were criticised by Lenin in *'Left-Wing' Communism, an Infantile Disorder* (1920) because of their opposition to communists participating in parliamentary elections and joining trade unions and Social Democratic Parties. The council communists split away from, or were expelled from, the Communist Parties of the Third International during the period 1920–1, and some of them organised alternative Communist Workers' Parties, such as the Communist Workers' Party of Germany (KAPD) in 1920. Sizeable council communist organisations disappeared as the post-war wave of radicalisation receded, and as the 1920s progressed the council communist movement was reduced to small groups engaged in theoretical work and propaganda activity. Paul Mattick's *Anti-Bolshevik Communism* (1978) represents some of the best fruits of the theoretical work in which the council communists have engaged.

BORDIGISM

Amadeo Bordiga and his comrades stood on the left wing of the Italian Socialist Party before the First World War and they were the most resolutely anti-war faction in Italy during the War. When the Communist Party of Italy was founded in 1921, the dominant position of Bordiga's faction within the new party was symbolised by the fact that Bordiga became the party leader. Bordiga had already been criticised by Lenin in *'Left-Wing' Communism, an Infantile Disorder* for advocating abstention from parliamentary elections, and in 1923 the executive committee of the Third International ousted him from the leadership of the Communist Party of Italy. Bordiga and his comrades remained within the Communist Party of Italy, but they suffered a defeat at the hands of Gramsci and his supporters, who were backed by the leaders of the Third International, at the congress held in exile in Lyons in 1926. Subsequently, the Bordigists either were expelled or withdrew from the Italian Communist Party, Bordiga himself being expelled in 1930. Although Bordiga was forced into political inactivity as long as Mussolini was in power, others who shared his views ensured that Bordigism maintained an organised existence. The form and name of the Bordigists' organisation changed at various junctures, but eventually became fixed as the International Communist Party, with members in Italy, France and elsewhere. Bordiga returned to political activity at the close of the Second World War and was associated with the International Communist Party until his death in 1970. Amadeo Bordiga's ideas on the nature of communist society have been presented in Jacques Camatte's *Bordiga et la passion du communisme* (1974).

SITUATIONISM

The situationists emerged in 1957 as a movement of avant-garde artists. Their criticism of consumer-oriented conventional art led them to criticise consumerism in general, and hence to attack the basis of capitalism – the production of wealth as commodities. Having widened their perspectives, their revolutionary activity principally took the form of publicity-catching stunts and the production of a stream of pamphlets and journals. Among their pamphlets, Guy Debord's *The Society of the Spectacle* (1967) and Raoul Vaneigem's *Traité de savoir-vivre à l'usage des jeunes générations* (1967) (translated into English as *The Revolution of Everyday Life*) are key texts. When tens of thousands of students and workers erupted onto the streets of Paris in May 1968, many of their protests had been anticipated by the situationists. Situationists were involved in the May events, but they never claimed to be leading the mass demonstrations and occupations, whose value they judged to lie in their spontaneity. From the 1970s, with the onset of economic depression, the situationists went into decline and were reduced to individuals and small groups engaged in propaganda activity.

From the foregoing, it can be seen that many of the chapters devote attention to organisations which have long since disbanded or to the ideas of people who are long since dead. We do not apologise for this. The theories which inspired these organisations and which were formulated by these people are relevant to the predicament in which the world finds itself today. Capitalism has not changed in any fundamental way since their day, and neither has the non-market socialist alternative to capitalism which they articulated.

Besides, although organisations and individuals may come and go, non-market socialism came into existence not long after industrial capitalism was established and has had a persistent, if chequered, history which extends down to the present day. The continued existence of non-market socialism is partly attributable to the efforts of those working men and women who have been its partisans, but paradoxically is due above all to the nature of capitalism itself. Capitalism necessarily entails an unceasing effort on the part of rival capitals throughout the world to maintain themselves by means of accumulation, and accumulation can only take place at the expense of the wage-working class. Unremitting exploitation and oppression of the wage-working class are built into capitalism, and can only be abolished by instituting a worldwide socialist society and hence destroying the implacable market forces which capitalism has unleashed. Thus it can confidently be said that as long as capitalism exists, the non-market socialist response to it will continually emerge within the working class.

Some people may be puzzled by the fact that we devote so much attention in this book to minority currents and less-than-famous individuals. How, it will be asked, can we neglect the mass movements of the past 100 years and their leaders?

Our response is to turn back the question to the questioners. Haven't the mass movements and their leaderships had their chances to right the wrongs of the world, by virtue of their attaining mass proportions? Conservatism, Liberalism, Social Democracy, Leninism . . . haven't they all had their share of power, and haven't they all proved totally ineffective in ridding the world of the problems which capitalism continually recreates? Other contenders for the privileges which accompany the administration of capitalism (nuclear disarmers, 'greens', feminists . . .) are waiting in the wings, and are having some success in turning themselves into mass movements because of the illusory attractiveness of their promises to reform the market system. Like previous attempts at reform, these latest efforts directed towards making the capitalist system function in a manner which gives priority to human interests are bound to fail. As long as the world market remains, human beings will be forced to dance to its tune. Market forces cannot be tamed; only eliminated. The very existence of humankind is now threatened by the rivalry and the fixation on profit which are inherent in the market system. Surely this is sufficient reason for setting aside preconceptions and prejudices and for considering the non-market socialists' case for abolishing the market on its intellectual and political merits.

As we have indicated, non-market socialism would necessarily be socialism on a world scale. In the society envisaged by non-market socialists, the people of the world would own the global means of production in common and would operate them communally for the benefit of humankind as a whole. Socialism in one country, or even one part of the world, is impossible. Since capitalism today is a global society which encompasses all parts of the world, the socialist alternative to capitalism must be equally global in its scope.

In view of the global nature of non-market socialism, it is appropriate that this book should be the result of an international effort by socialists who live in a number of countries. Nevertheless, it has to be admitted that all the contributors live in advanced, industrialised countries and that the focus of most chapters is primarily European. This is perhaps inevitable, given the facts that capitalism first developed in Europe and that, as a result, the non-market socialist response to capitalism also originated in Europe. The various currents of non-market socialism which are discussed in Chapters 3 to 7 all first emerged in Europe, although some of them have since spread to other continents.

Despite the European backgrounds of the various contributors, however, it is important to emphasise that the message of this book is not Euro-centrist. Non-market socialism is as relevant to the plight of those who are starving in Africa and other parts of the world as it is to the inhabitants of London or Paris. It is true that non-market socialists have generally seen the wage workers of those advanced, industrialised areas of the world which act as the power-houses of international capitalism (Europe, North America and Japan) as the force which is likely to initiate the revolutionary change from world capitalism to world socialism. Yet the establishment of non-market socialism could not be accomplished without the active cooperation of the majority of the population in those parts of the world which capitalism has consigned to underdevelopment. In contrast to the hopelessness and destitution which afflict the majority of the people in backward countries under world capitalism, the prospect of dignity and sufficiency which world socialism would open up for them would be overwhelmingly attractive. It is also worth mentioning that several of the non-market socialist principles which are identified in Chapter 2 closely resemble the principles of social cooperation found among hunter-gatherers and other supposedly 'backward' people. People in their social position would take much less convincing of the desirability of non-market socialism than would many of those in 'advanced' countries who are currently steeped in the values and assumptions which capitalism encourages.

Non-market socialism would be a global solution to the global problems which have accompanied the rise of world capitalism.

1 Non-Market Socialism in the Nineteenth Century

Maximilien Rubel

I

For hundreds of millions of people today the words 'socialism' and 'communism' are synonymous with a state-controlled economy and with state dictatorship. What sense can there be, therefore, in wanting to show that in the beginning these terms meant human communities in which every individual, with all the richness of his or her particular nature, could live and develop freely and harmoniously, so that none would be subject to the material and moral constraints inherent in the systems of production and domination as a whole which characterise our twentieth century?

What can we, who are just small groups of well-intentioned people, hope to gain by obstinately conserving and cultivating the original meaning of these two words, when we know that there is no chance that our semantic faithfulness will modify a state of affairs that has been sanctified by the usage of officially legitimised 'socialist' and 'communist' propaganda machines? It would be useless to deny that our way of thinking resembles that of religious believers, with the difference that the latter accept the religious dogmas defended by their churches as truths revealed by sacred texts and do not contrast the original doctrines and early martyrs with the established institutions and present-day officials of their churches, whereas we refuse to recognise the claims of the leaders of self-styled socialist and communist regimes to such legitimacy. The comparison may be taken even further: for example, we could categorise ourselves as 'primitive believers', like those contemporary Christians who condemn all organised churches, accusing them of having betrayed the spirit of the Evangelists, and who strive to follow faithfully the teachings of their Saviour. These Christians can base themselves on historical evidence which proves that sects like themselves have actually existed and have been persecuted for following the commandments of their mythical ideal. But what can we, who cultivate the purity of the original ideas of socialism and communism, do other than invoke the nineteenth-century socialist authors and their theories, even though their generous ideas and promises of liberation have never been put into practice in large- or even small-scale model communities?

Our twentieth century has witnessed the construction of empires which are universally recognised as 'socialist', until the point has been reached where they are considered by many specialists (of Sovietology or Sinology or . . Marxology) to incarnate the 'communist world system'. We, on the contrary, consider all this to be simply a monstrous perversion of the language and the idea from which the first great projects for social transformation arose. Because there is continual talk about 'real socialism' and 'actually existing socialism', our objective is to revolt against this sociologically explicable, yet morally intolerable, abuse and to invent new terms and expressions while trying to conserve the corrupted words and names, as if such semantic fidelity were a determinant factor in the outcome of the revolutionary movement which we hope and fight for.

In a word, because we consider ourselves 'true' communists and socialists, we want to proclaim our difference from the 'false' socialists and communists, at the risk of being taken in by our own verbal game and conceding a certain mysterious affinity with our opponents. Hence a number of the contributors to this book have proposed to designate our conception of social theory – we might even say social creed – as 'non-market socialism'.

The immediate objection that we can expect to this is the following: you reduce the conception of socialism to one criterion, i.e., the absence of the *market*, or more precisely, the absence of the *market economy*. In adopting this purely negative criterion, you lay claim to a whole field of reflection in order to establish the positive characteristics of your non-market socialism. However, this way of reasoning amounts to attributing a residue of socialism, a mysterious socialist market-negating quality, to the falsely socialist and truly capitalist (state-capitalist) regimes. Thus, the USSR would in some way be founded on 'market socialism', so that it would suffice to eliminate the market to establish 'true socialism', that original socialism as understood in the nineteenth century and – why not? – during the era of the 1917 Russian Revolution.

But are we not falling into a kind of Neo-Scholasticism, involved as we are, in a metaphysical debate over the relation between essence and appearance (*Wesen* and *Schein*) or between being and nothingness (*Sein* and *Nichts*)? In short, are we not seeking, without full consciousness of our acts, to find shelter in what Spinoza called the 'asylum of ignorance' that is so warmly appreciated by the devotees of religious superstitions?

II

The term 'socialism', which dates from the third decade of the last century, was used by various authors and militants throughout the whole period up until the beginning of the twentieth century to describe principally those social projects which encompassed both imaginary elements and reform proposals that could be realised in the short term, if not at once. Thus, the distinction invented by Friedrich Engels between 'utopian' and 'scientific' socialism does not seem to correspond exactly to the real situation of great intellectual complexity, where products of the imagination flourished side-by-side with the fruits of rational and pragmatic reflection. This mixture of dream and science is present in Marx's work, as it was in the works of his predecessors and teachers. We should never forget that Marx was also the author of the renowned *Economic and Philosophic Manuscripts of 1844*.[1] Of all the nineteenth-century social reformers, Marx appears as the most consistent theorist of 'non-market socialism', even if, after Marx, a particular school of anarchism (often in ignorance of Marx's theoretical contribution) was able to enrich with a revolutionary dimension the heritage of socialism and communism in all their variants, in such a way that today we are obliged to call into question many of the principles of so-called scientific socialism. (See Chapter 3.)

Theoretically speaking, the Marxian conception of socialism is identical with the negation of the market economy, in contrast to the other socialist doctrines, before and after Marx, which conserve in varying ways certain aspects of the capitalist mode of production and distribution. We need only recall those pages of the *Communist Manifesto* devoted to 'socialist and communist literature' to see that the authors did not hesitate to employ expressions made up of apparently contradictory elements, as if the noun 'socialism' could be harnessed with any adjective without the risk of falling into the trap of a *contradictio in adjecto*:

I. Reactionary Socialism
  a. Feudal Socialism
  b. Petty-Bourgeois Socialism
  c. German, or 'True', Socialism
II. Conservative, or Bourgeois, Socialism
III. Critical-Utopian Socialism and Communism[2]

In agreeing to discuss a subject such as 'non-market socialism', and thus implicitly approving the creation of this neologism, we are indeed placing ourselves in the tradition of the *Manifesto*, but, at the same time, we are recognising the existence not of a particular *literature*, unknown to Marx and Engels, but of a *socio-economic reality* which others call 'market socialism'.

III

The remarkable thing in the above listing is its more or less total rejection of the first two forms of socialism (Reactionary and Conservative, or Bourgeois types of Socialism) on the one hand, and its quite positive appreciation of the third (Critical-Utopian Socialism and Communism) on the other. As far as our topic is concerned, we can affirm that this classification opposes the adepts of 'market socialism' to those of a 'non-market socialism'. These adepts are represented by a small number of authors, some of whom are mentioned by name, while others although unnamed are relatively easy to guess. No name is mentioned in the passage on 'Feudal Socialism', where the aristocracies of France and England are discussed and it is indicated that a 'section of the French Legitimists and "Young England"' represent those 'feudalists' who 'forget that they exploited under circumstances and conditions that were quite different, and that are now antiquated'.[3] The probable targets here are figures such as Chateaubriand for France and Thomas Carlyle for England. On the other hand, it seems improbable that when Marx and Engels proceeded in the same passage to evoke 'Christian Socialism', they were thinking of an author such as Félicité R. de Lamennais, the former priest and apostate, whose works *Paroles d'un croyant* (1833), *Le Livre du peuple* (1838) and *De l'Esclavage moderne* (1839) aroused more echoes in all Europe than . . . the *Communist Manifesto*. Lamennais's thought, a mixture of primitive Christianity and Saint-Simonism tinged with Jacobinism, is rich in that ethical spirit without which the socialist and communist proclamations are nothing more than phraseology and a pretext for dissimulating a will to power and therefore exploitation.

As to the second form of 'Reactionary Socialism', defined as 'Petty-Bourgeois Socialism', the 1848 *Manifesto* gives us only one name, that of Sismondi, about whom it is said that he 'was the head of this school, not only in France but also in England'.[4] But if this school is criticised chiefly for its attachment to the 'old means of production and of exchange, and with them the old property relations',[5] it receives high praise in return:

> This school of Socialism dissected with great acuteness the contradictions in the conditions of modern production. It laid bare the hypocritical apologies of economists. It proved, incontrovertibly, the disastrous effects of machinery and division of labour; the concentration of capital and land in a few hands; over-production and crises; it pointed out the inevitable ruin of the petty bourgeois and peasant, the misery of the proletariat, the anarchy in production, the crying inequalities in the distribution of wealth, the industrial war of extermination between nations, the dissolution of old moral bonds, of the old family relations, of the old nationalities.[6]

In a word, Sismondi and his school, while advocating a sort of reactionary and utopian 'market socialism', anticipated through their critical theory of the capitalist mode of production the theorists of so-called scientific socialism!

Finally, we come to the third form of 'Reactionary Socialism', about which the authors of the *Manifesto* express an unconditionally negative verdict, without however suggesting any names. This passage reads like a condensed version of the polemic that Marx and Engels developed in the voluminous manuscript of the *German Ideology* (1846–7) against 'True Socialism'.[7] The second volume of the work bore the subtitle 'True Socialism', and there we find severe critiques of several articles which had appeared in the *Rheinischen Jahrbücher* (vol. I, 1845), a periodical that was representative of the 'philosophy of true socialism'. One chapter, which undoubtedly stemmed from Marx's hand, is directed against Karl Grün, author of an anthology of essays entitled *Die soziale Bewegung in Frankreich und Belgien* (1845).[8] Marx attacks this 'historiography of true socialism', and in doing so shows his mastery of both contemporary and classic socialist and communist literature (i.e. Moses Hess, Proudhon, Louis Blanc, Cabet, etc. for the contemporaries, and Condorcet, Babeuf, Morelly, Saint-Simon, Fourier for the classics). In so doing, Marx made thorough use of two sources: *Les Etudes sur les réformateurs ou socialistes modernes* (1840) by Louis Reybaud, as well as Lorenz Stein's *Der Socialismus und Communismus des heutigen Frankreichs* (1842).

The global judgement formulated in the *Manifesto* against 'German or True socialism' should interest us here since it implies the recognition of the historical necessity of liberal-bourgeois and therefore capitalist civilisation, and consequently, 'market socialism'. It is now our task to examine the second and third categories of socialist and communist literature ('Conservative, or Bourgeois, Socialism' and 'Critical-Utopian Socialism and Communism'), where the essential aspects of 'non-market socialism' are presented to us both through the critique of bourgeois reformism and through the partial appropriation of the positive propositions bequeathed by the inventors of socialist and communist utopias.

IV

Following the three forms of 'Reactionary Socialism', in the passage devoted to 'Conservative, or Bourgeois, Socialism' a sole author stands as the scapegoat for all the 'bourgeois socialists': Pierre-Joseph Proudhon. Only one of Proudhon's books is cited: *Le Système des contradictions économiques, ou Philosophie de la misère* (1846).[9] We know that Proudhon expected to feel the lash of Marx's criticism for having hesitated to join the ongoing project of communist propaganda,[10] and that this work, of tedious verbosity, had provoked the expected response in the form of a skilful pamphlet by Marx entitled *Misère de la philosophie* (1847).[11] The *Manifesto* limits itself to repeating several formulas developed at length in Marx's response. However, these few critical remarks amount essentially to the statement that Proudhonian socialism:

> sought to depreciate every revolutionary movement in the eyes of the working class, by showing that no mere political reform, but only a change in the material conditions of existence, in economical relations, could be of any advantage to them. By changes in the material conditions of existence, this form of Socialism, however, by no means understands abolition of the bourgeois relations of production, an abolition that can be effected only by a revolution, but administrative reforms, based on the continued existence of these relations; reforms, therefore, that in no respect affect the relations between capital and labour, but, at the best, lessen the cost, and simplify the administrative work, of bourgeois government.[12]

In short, Marx reduces the Proudhonian teaching to the dimensions of a 'market socialism' *sui generis*, while heaping reproach on his antagonist for opposing the revolutionary and political movement of the modern-day proletariat. What is perhaps surprising in Marx's unconditional critique of Proudhon's system is that he seems little inclined to repeat the smallest fragment of the high praise that he had expressed three years earlier for the genial worker who had written the *Mémoire sur la propriété*.[13]

V

Turning to the third and last category in the *Manifesto*'s outline of socialism, we find an intellectual climate which is closest to the conception of 'non-market socialism' as we are trying to define it. If we examine attentively the comments which the *Manifesto* reserves for 'Critical-Utopian Socialism and Communism', we must now admit that in certain respects the critiques made of the great utopians seem to be *more utopian* than the often chimerical systems of someone like Saint-Simon, Fourier or Owen, to take the three founders of 'Socialist and Communist systems' who are mentioned in particular as representative of both the virtues and the vices of utopia.

The passage on 'Critical-Utopian Socialism and Communism' begins with a negative proposition that is somewhat enigmatic:

> We do not here refer to that literature which, in every great modern revolution, has always given voice to the demands of the proletariat, such as the writings of Babeuf and others.[14]

What are we to understand by this evident praise not for Babeuf the *actor* (and for others like him?) but for Babeuf the *writer*, the publicist, and more or less exclusive editor of several papers, the most famous of which was *Le Tribun du peuple ou le Défenseur des droits de l'homme* (October 1794–April 1796)? To be sure, the figure of Babeuf the revolutionary, guillotined by the Thermidorians after the discovery of the 'conspiracy of Equals' (1797), fits badly into the gallery of 'critical-utopians' who:

> reject all political, and especially all revolutionary, action; they wish to attain their ends by peaceful means, and endeavour, by small experiments, necessarily doomed to failure, and by the force of example, to pave the way for the new social Gospel.[15]

In short, the *Manifesto* distinguishes clearly between a literature whose inspiration is political and revolutionary and a literary production whose only merit is its critical and inventive spirit. Yet we may rightly affirm that both schools of socialism share a common aim: the negation of the market economy; thus both represent the theoretical conception that we designate with the neologism 'non-market socialism'. Did the authors of the *Manifesto* situate themselves in the tradition of Babeuf because of its political character, in other words chiefly for having found there what we might call a transitional project which was realistic enough to have a chance of fulfilling the preconditions or premises of non-market socialism? This hypothesis is all the more plausible for being backed up by a text by Marx which pre-dates the *Manifesto* and which serves as a warning to the makers of ideas and theories, and therefore, in a way, it concerns us as well, we who do our utmost to propagate 'true socialism' . . . The following is a meaningful passage taken from *The Holy Family* (1845):

> *Ideas* can never lead beyond an old world order but only beyond the ideas of the old world order. Ideas *cannot carry out anything* at all. In order to carry out ideas men are needed who can exert practical force . . . the French Revolution gave rise to ideas which led beyond the *ideas* of the entire old world order. The revolutionary movement which began in 1789 in the *Cercle social*, which in the middle of its course had as its chief representatives *Leclerc* and *Roux*, and which finally with *Babeuf*'s conspiracy was temporarily defeated, gave rise to the *communist* idea which *Babeuf*'s friend *Buonarroti* re-introduced in France after the Revolution of 1830. This idea, consistently developed, is the *idea* of the *new world order.*[16]

VI

The *Manifesto* discovers this 'idea of the new world order' in, or attributes it to, the famous inventors of socialist and communist systems, among whom we obviously find the great triumvirate of utopianism, the three authors who in fact were very different, if not indeed opposed in many respects: Saint-Simon, Fourier and Owen. A fourth author can be recognised, although he is left unmentioned: Etienne Cabet, about whom the *Manifesto* ironises in recalling his *Voyage en Icarie* (1842), but above all, it attacks the epigones of the first three, those disciples who 'have, in every case, formed mere reactionary sects'.[17] Their teachers, however, despite their lack of comprehension of the 'historical self-praxis' of the modern proletariat, were the first to express a radical critique of the existing social organisation. Moreover, they set up projects for social transformation which are rational anticipations of the future human community:

> They attack every principle of existing society. Hence they are full of the most valuable materials for the enlightenment of the working class. The practical measures proposed in them – such as the abolition of the distinction between town and country, of the family, of the carrying on of industries for the account of private individuals, and of the wage system, the proclamation of social harmony, the conversion of the functions of the State into a mere superintendence of production, all these proposals point solely to the disappearance of class-antagonisms which were, at that time, only just cropping up, and which, in these publications, are recognised in their earliest indistinct and undefined forms only. These proposals, therefore, are of a purely Utopian character.[18]

To the extent that we have an agreed definition of 'non-market socialism', we would probably find that it encompassed all or at least most of the 'practical measures' presented in the above list. However, what we now have to do is first to complete the *Manifesto*'s much too schematic table of the literature which is capable of informing our conception of non-market socialism and, second, enquire as to the validity, in the times and the world we are living in, of the critical remarks formulated in the 1848 *Manifesto* against the inventors of socialist and communist utopias.

With regard to the former, I shall limit myself to recalling two documents stemming from Marx. As for the latter, I should like to outline a mode of adaptation of the 1848 critiques to today's situation.

VII

In 1845 Marx and Engels elaborated an editorial project to publish, in German, a 'Library of the Best Foreign Socialist Writers'. This project never materialised, but in the unpublished papers of both men we find a number of notes by

Marx and a fragmentary text by Engels. Below is a plan outline, written in March 1845, which is found in one of Marx's notebooks for the period 1844–7 (the arrangement of the names follows a certain logic, while at the same time respecting approximately their chronological order):[19]

Morelly
Mably
Babeuf
Buonarroti

Cercle soc[ial]
Hébert
Jac[ques] Roux
Leclerc

Bentham
Godwin

[d']Holbach
Fourier

Owen
(Lalande)

Helvétius
S[ain]t-Simon

Considérant
Cabet
'Fraternité', l'égalitaire, etc.
l'humanitaire
Proudhon

Producteur. Globe

Writings of the School
Dézamy. Gay.
and X

It is not difficult to guess which of the above-mentioned writers are considered by Marx and Engels as being the spokesmen of proletarian demands, given their selective treatment in the *Communist Manifesto*. Note that, apart from the names of authors, Marx put down a few newspaper titles, organs of secret societies inspired by Babeuf whose members were mainly workers. It is not without interest that several of the above-named authors are also mentioned in a section of the *Holy Family* entitled 'Critical Battle against French Materialism', in which Marx took a strong stand on 'the connection of eighteenth-century materialism with English and French *communism* of the nineteenth century'[20] after having stressed the relationship, in these authors, between materialism and the *communist ethic*:

Fourier proceeds directly from the teaching of the French materialists. The *Babouvists* were crude, uncivilised materialists, but developed communism, too, derives *directly* from *French materialism*. The latter returned to its mother-country, *England*, in the form *Helvétius* gave it. *Bentham* based his system of *correctly understood interest* on Helvétius' morality, and *Owen* proceeded from *Bentham*'s system to found English communism. Exiled to England, the Frenchman *Cabet* came under the influence of communist ideas there and on his return to France became the most popular, if the most superficial, representative of communism. Like Owen, the more scientific French Communists, *Dézamy*, *Gay* and others, developed the teaching of *materialism* as the teaching of *real humanism* and the *logical* basis of *communism*.[21]

Again, in relation to the third section of the *Communist Manifesto*, Marx left a draft plan on the cover of a notebook containing the manuscript on 'Wages' (written in Brussels, December 1847).[22] At that time Marx was preparing to write the *Manifesto*, as he had been charged to do at the second congress of the Communist League in London. This draft plan reads as follows:

First Draft

1) [Critique][23] Critical Utopian Systems (Communist).
2)

Second Draft

1) Reactionary socialism, feudal, religious petty bourgeois.
2) Bourgeois socialism.
3) German philosophical socialism.
4) Critical utopian systems of literature. Owen, Cabet, Weitling, Fourier, S[ain]t-Simon, Babeuf.
5) Direct party literature.
6) Communist literature.[24]

What stands out in this plan is the presence of the name of Wilhelm Weitling, the workman-tailor for whom Marx had first shown true veneration to the point where he valued his works more than those of Proudhon, while Engels called him the 'founder of German Communism'.[25] A political confrontation in the communist group in Belgium between Marx and

Weitling caused Marx to forget that he once saw in the author of *Garantien der Harmonie und Freiheit* (1842) the personification of the athletic figure of the German proletariat.[26] While items 1 to 4 correspond almost word for word to the survey in the *Manifesto*, topics 5 and 6 are not dealt with. It would be interesting to find the names and writings that Marx thought to mention there, especially since we now know practically all the revolutionary literature which he studied prior to 1848. We might imagine, for instance, that he would have given his opinion on the contribution of Louis Blanc, Pierre Leroux and also perhaps Auguste Blanqui, among others. We should not forget to add to this list of masculine names, those of two women, Flora Tristan and George Sand. It would have been easier for us to reconstitute the Marxian conception of 'non-market socialism' with the aid of 'Direct party' and 'Communist' literature, duly commented on by Marx.

VIII

Today, more than a century after Marx's death, after more than a hundred years of *Marx-Streit*, of quarrels over the 'real' Marx, after more than six decades of Marxism's victory as a state ideology, what can we say about the severe criticisms of the utopians formulated in the *Manifesto*, and above all, what can we say about the assurance with which the two authors opposed to social Utopias ('duodecimo editions of the New Jerusalem')[27] the alleged *reality* of a working-class movement or a social movement whose chances of success appeared to them to be absolutely certain, as if they were dealing with a tangible and evident phenomenon? In particular, we should not neglect the so-called 'scientific' assurance which lay behind remarks such as the following:

> All previous [historical, 1888 edn] movements were movements of minorities, or in the interest of minorities. The proletarian movement is [!] the self-conscious, independent movement of the immense [!] majority, in the interest of the immense majority. The proletariat, the lowest stratum of our present society, cannot stir, cannot raise itself up, without the whole superincumbent strata of official society being sprung into the air.[28]

This hypothesis – so dogmatically opposed to the utopians – is logical only if we set the verbs in the future instead of the present tense, or in the normative instead of the indicative: the proletarian movement *will be*, or *ought to be*, the self-conscious, independent movement of the immense majority . . and so on. Who could affirm, without inviting ridicule, that in the time of Marx and Engels, when utopia was still prospering, the working-class movement actually showed the characteristics that the *Manifesto* attributed to it? This question is even more important if we formulate it with regard to our own era, when no trace of any such working-class movement is perceptible! The historical initiative, the 'historical self-praxis' of the proletariat remains, today as well as yesterday, a *postulate*, or even a *hypothesis*, or – and on this point my way of thinking may well offend all vulgar materialists, whether Marxist or not – simply an *ethical imperative*. In addition, the present-day proletariat, especially in the economically developed countries, bears little resemblance to that of the nineteenth century and does not seem sufficiently advanced in an intellectual sense to grasp the profound and original meaning of socialist and communist thought, whether this be Karl Marx's anarcho-socialism[29] or the non-market socialism that we are in the process of inventing.

The criticisms levelled at the utopians were not really justified in 1848, any more than they are justified today:

> Future history resolves itself, in their eyes, into the propaganda and the practical carrying out of their social plans.
>
> In the formation of their plans they are conscious of caring chiefly for the interests of the working class, as being the most suffering class. Only from the point of view of being the most suffering class does the proletariat exist for them.[30]

The situation is basically the same today as it was then; the crises inherent in the nature of capital have assumed, in the twentieth century, the most barbarous forms, as science and technology have evolved to attain new heights. The degree of suffering inflicted on the virtual totality of our species is proportional to the level of wonders produced in all the fields of science and technique. It is this situation, as it were, that Marx described towards the end of volume I of *Capital*, but solely as it concerns the negative, destructive effects of capital accumulation. Marx, the man of science, ably grasped this 'negative' aspect of capitalism when he asserted:

> Along with the constantly diminishing number of the magnates of capital, who usurp and monopolise all advantages of this process of transformation, grows the mass of misery, oppression, slavery, degradation, exploitation.[31]

However, when he added,

> but with this too grows the revolt of the working-class, a class always increasing in numbers, and disciplined, united, organised by the very mechanism of the process of capitalist production itself[32]

we are no longer in the field of empirical, and thus scientific, observation, in the usual sense of the term, but once again, as with the expressions used in the *Manifesto*, in the sphere of normative judgements, and thus of *ethics*.

The first person who questioned the scientific nature of chapter 32 of *Capital* (from which the above quotations are taken) was Georges Sorel, and he was also the first to consider it as the conclusion of the whole work, although Marx had placed it *before* chapter 33, which deals with 'The Modern Theory of Colonization'. Sorel thought that Marx had simply inserted the four pages on the 'Historical Tendency of Capitalist Accumulation' which constitute chapter 32, and which were written well before the book, perhaps around 1847, to express 'the diverse hypotheses that prevail in his conception of the future'.[33] A discerning reader, Sorel then put his view into words that we would do well to reflect on in our search for an acceptable definition of 'non-market socialism':

> Taken literally, this *apocalyptic text* has no great interest; if it is interpreted as a product of the mind, as an image constructed with a view to developing consciousness, then it certainly is the conclusion of *Capital* and is a good *illustration* of the principles on which Marx thought it necessary to base the rules of the proletariat's socialist action.[34]

If Sorel had used the word 'ethical' to characterise this concluding chapter of *Capital* instead of 'apocalyptic', he would have shown himself to be more consistent, especially since he had already broached this topic in a lecture on 'The Ethics of Socialism'.[35]

But let Marx continue his reasoning in the anticipative indicative:

> The monopoly of capital becomes a fetter upon the mode of production, which has sprung up and flourished along with, and under it. Centralisation of the means of production and socialisation of labour at last reach a point where they become incompatible with their capitalist integument. This integument is burst asunder. The knell of capitalist private property sounds. The expropriators are expropriated.[36]

This avouched 'flirt' with the Hegelian dialectic should not prevent us from understanding the 'negation of the negation' not as a law of nature, but as an ethical norm and a political exhortation addressed to modern slaves with a view to creating the new City, the harmonious society, non-market socialism. This is our way of refuting the critical argument over Marx's so-called economism, as if some mysterious providence had decreed the automatism of human emancipation. Let us try to read the last lines of *Capital* as an invitation to a practice oriented less towards inventing new theories or new socialist epithets than towards propagating teachings inherited, it is true, from the past, but still and perpetually open to an indeterminate future, and therefore relevant to that 'poetry of the future' that Marx recommended to the nineteenth-century revolutionaries:

> The transformation of scattered private property, arising from individual labour, into capitalist private property is, naturally, a process, incomparably more protracted, violent, and difficult, than the transformation of capitalistic private property, already practically resting on socialised production, into socialised property. In the former case, we had the expropriation of the mass of the people by a few usurpers; in the latter, we have the expropriation of a few usurpers by the mass of the people.[37]

It is significant that appended to this epilogue is a footnote quoting the 1848 *Manifesto*, where we already find the deterministic formula on account of which Marx has repeatedly been reproached, since it is said to furnish proof of his . . . profane messianism:

> What the bourgeoisie, therefore, produces, above all, are its own grave-diggers. Its fall and the victory of the proletariat are equally inevitable.[38]

IX

Within the limits of this discussion, it is scarcely possible to try to analyse the movement of ideas which, following Marx's death, contributed to the tradition of non-market socialism. The damage wrought by the double mystification, Marxist and anti-Marxist, was such that it gave rise to the image of Marx as an 'authoritarian socialist', a 'state communist', rather than the conception of Marx's work as, despite its incomplete state, the first to develop a *theory of anarchy*. This conception appears to be even less acceptable today than it ever was, since the 1917 Russian Revolution succeeded, thanks to Lenin and his party, in forcing itself upon the consciousness of the masses as the first 'socialist' revolution guided by 'scientific Marxism'. In his moments of lucidity and intellectual honesty, Lenin preferred to admit that the economic system of the new Russia resembled state capitalism more than any form of socialism. As a diligent reader of *Capital*, Lenin was able to find there one single 'recipe for the cook-shops of the future'; this was the recipe for the best method of creating an immense proletariat, *ergo* an immense capitalist economy, *ergo* a repressive state apparatus, *ergo* an extraordinary means for making Marxism an instrument of ideological mystification.

I deny either the accuracy or the usefulness of interpreting the system based on the 'Soviet' model as a form of 'market socialism'. On the contrary, I am inclined to characterise the mode of production in the Russia of the *non*-Soviets as *non-market capitalism*, and I even maintain that the so-called socialist planning in fact plans not the *abundance* of goods but their *scarcity*. In this regard, may I remind you that the first sentence of *Capital* reads as follows:

> The wealth of those societies in which the capitalist mode of production prevails, presents itself as 'an immense accumulation of commodities', its unit being a single commodity.[39]

There is no need to be an economist to see that those societies whose oligarchies have succeeded in convincing the public in general, and even the liberal-minded Western intelligentsia and a whole school of Marxists, that they administer both a 'socialist' economy and a 'socialist' state are in reality societies which are subject to the laws of a hybrid mode of production, half feudal/half capitalist. They are characterised, to differing degrees, by an economy of scarcity, not an economy of abundance, and as such they do not have the same features that Marx observed in the developed capitalist countries, which are quite obviously 'market capitalist societies'. Had Lenin modelled his convictions in accordance with Marx's social theory, he would have clearly admitted that he and his party were called upon to exercise dictatorial power not in order to accomplish the historical mission of the proletariat but in order to fulfil the vocation of a bourgeoisie which had been destroyed in Russia. Furthermore, he would have drawn the final inferences from this train of thought, if he had announced the coming of the gravediggers of the feudal-bourgeois Bolshevism which he had succeeded in imposing on his country in the mystifying garb of Marxist ideology. As the negation of Tsarism, Bolshevism created the material conditions for the negation of the negation, for the expropriation of the expropriators. Having transformed the peasantry into proletariat – as Marx had foreseen should Russian populism (the *narodničestvo*) be defeated – the party of Lenin, Trotsky and Stalin, to name just the chief agitators, gradually changed into a historical instrument for primitive and enlarged capital accumulation, a process which does not yet seem to have been accomplished except for the successful accumulation of nuclear armaments and other commodities of destruction.

All this ought to seem less paradoxical if we look at what occurred in post-1917 Russia with the eyes of consistent materialists and reach a judgement based on the real circumstances and conditions which prevailed and not according to the claims of the protagonists themselves, whose mentality of lords and masters is more akin to the spirit of eighteenth- and nineteenth-century capitalism than to the creative imagination of the utopians, including Marx. Behind their communist discourse we find the ambition of the pioneers of market capitalism, with the difference that for Russia in 1917, caught up in the pangs of national and civil war, the first priority was given to creating the material conditions for survival, without undertaking a strictly market policy of profit accumulation. After the period of 'war communism', with its phenomena of famine and cannibalism, the long period of economic reconstruction began, with the elaboration of a system of non-market capitalism, of planned state capitalism. Its theory was elaborated, contradictorily, in the well-known 'industrial debates', with the necessary recourse to the classical Marxist categories of the market economy (commodities, capital, wages, profit and so on), which were verbosely idealised with the aid of the adjectives 'socialist' and 'communist'. Thus, the concept of 'capitalist accumulation' was transformed into 'socialist accumulation' and so forth. The supreme court of Marxist ideologists did not fear being unmasked by the peasant and working-class masses, who were freed from the despotism of the tsars and who engaged in actions of spontaneous expropriation enthusiastically but without a thought for theory and ideology. In harnessing and recuperating this emancipatory will of the peasant and working-class masses, who were the real actors of the Russian Revolution, the Bolshevik Party acted unconsciously as if its historical task was to give birth to a modern capitalist Russia and obeyed more or less instinctively the determinism that Marx so strikingly defined in the Preface to *Capital*:

> And even when a society has got upon the right track for the discovery of the natural laws of its movement – and it is the ultimate aim of this work, to lay bare the economic law of motion of modern society – it can neither clear by bold leaps, nor remove by legal enactments, the obstacles offered by the successive phases of its normal development. But it can shorten and lessen the birth-pangs.[40]

The multisecular backwardness of Russian society with respect to the material civilisation of the West persuaded the Bolshevik oligarchy to select and implement a policy for accelerating the transformation of their empire by intensifying the protracted and relatively less barbarous birth-pangs that the Western nations had been subjected to for centuries.

CONCLUSION

If we choose to call ourselves 'non-market socialists', even though we are conscious of the pleonasm incorporated into this form of words, the reason is that we do not wish to run the risk of associating ourselves politically and intellectually with a politico-economic system that is socialist only in name. Nevertheless, it could be said that our choice, in this case, is based on a terminological specification that lacks any logical foundation. Furthermore, it might be argued that we risk giving the impression that we take seriously a mystification which not only avails itself of a simply delusive ideology, but which has helped to develop an oligarchical regime that disposes of all the modern means of domination and exploitation. It is not so much the existence of the 'market' that authorises us to reject 'market socialism' as non-socialist and forces us to look for a new term to differentiate ourselves from it. It would be more logical to refer to our conception of socialism by retaining the original terminology, but this logic would tend to spread confusion, since the pseudo-socialist regimes have been completely successful in gaining official and non-official recognition as the managers of 'real socialism'. The bourgeois oligarchies have every interest in letting themselves be mystified, in order to praise the virtues of liberal capitalism in the light of 'gulag socialism'.

Even in the nineteenth century, the word 'socialism' was not synonymous with 'non-market socialism', and Marx's utopian-scientific socialism was the only *theory* of the radical negation of money and the state. At the same time, it adopted a *practice of transition* that may be qualified as 'realistic' because it is determined by the interaction between development of the productive forces and development of proletarian mentalities. Condemning utopian micro-experiences, while recognising their relative importance from a critical and imaginative point of view, Marx shut himself up in the kingdom of utopia and imagined rather than observed a revolutionary movement carried forward by 'the immense majority in the interest of the immense majority'. Since, more than one hundred years after Marx, we are still in the process of imagining and awaiting the mass revolt of the modern helots, we not only have the right but also the moral obligation of maintaining the tradition of a rational utopia. Similarly, as wage-earners with an educative calling, we should give the example of a *political* praxis whose objective is to unite all revolutionary tendencies and whose aim is the creation of that planetary community foreseen by the poets of utopia.

'The superman is a premature ideal that supposes the existence of man.'[41] This aphorism from Karl Kraus expresses perfectly the sense of the socialist, communist and anarchist theory and practice for which we are seeking a new name in our perplexity, our fear and horror of the barbarity that is the 'leprosy of civilisation'. Must we really engage in a verbal search which hides an almost religious nostalgia? Our model thinkers of the nineteenth century knew much less about the rhythm of human evolution than we know not only since Lamarck, Champollion, Boucher de Perthes and Darwin, but above all since the recent discoveries in molecular biology; as against a duration of some thirty million years for the anthropomorphous apes, *Homo sapiens* dates back only 30 000 years. Biologically speaking, the human species is young and seems to have before it a future of several hundreds of thousands of years. Fighting against natural selection, the human species invents means of selection such as ethnocide, war, genocide and nuclear arms; the human species has thus acquired the technical and moral possibility of destroying itself, while destroying all trace of life on earth.

Such is the language of the new biologist and 'new philosopher'. The 'non-market socialist' thinks not only in generic terms but also in socio-political concepts. Instead of *Man*, he sees hundreds of generations of men and women living in class societies where the 'immense majority' submits to the yoke of minorities athirst for power and prestige, oligarchies whose members share, beyond their politico-cultural divergencies, a morbid instinct for domination. Today, in the age of electronics, cybernetics and nuclear arms, these oligarchies are stricken with *politico-military paranoia*. Not by indulging in new epithets do we remain faithful to our pursuit of a new world. Let us work together instead on a practice of dissidence and reformist-revolutionary transition, while enriching and perfecting the intellectual legacy we have inherited from the nineteenth century.

By Way of a Bibliography

The foregoing text, conceived as an introduction to a debate on what we have agreed to call 'non-market socialism', is necessarily incomplete. Constraints of space have forced me to omit the names and ideas of the lesser known, pre-Marxian authors who not only advanced a critical analysis of the social institutions created by the capitalist economy, but also had a vision of what Robert Owen called 'the New Moral World'. Even so, it would not be enough simply to list the contributions of nineteenth-century authors to a theory of non-market socialism. This would be to neglect the intellectual endeavours and the subversive efforts of several generations of manual workers. E. P. Thompson defined his book on *The Making of the English Working Class* 'as a biography of the English working class from its adolescence until its early manhood'. He specified that 'In the years between 1780 and 1832 most English working people came to feel an identity of interests as between themselves, and as against their rulers and employers.'[42] By so doing, he incites us to reflect on similar events and phenomena in countries other than Great Britain.

Of course, even if some of us are labelled 'professional intellectuals', this is no guarantee of the seriousness and consequently the usefulness of our work. Nevertheless, our task would be simple indeed if all it consisted of was to help bring about the revolution which we dream of by making known the ideas, theories and projects which collectively constitute a theory worthy of the name of non-market socialism. In reality, we are far from accomplishing even this much. Yet all the while the established oligarchies are engaged in multiplying the mass media, which serve as so many instruments for the mental degradation of those whom the *Communist Manifesto* perceived not only as the 'immense majority' but even as the mainstream of a great emancipatory movement. Proposing this list of works to be consulted, I would like to imagine that some day we will be capable of countering the so-called democratic and bourgeois (but in fact stupefying) mass media by means of a periodical which will achieve a mass readership. Such a periodical would need to recall the ideas of liberation which have existed in all eras, and to do so in a style of language which would be accessible to anyone capable of reading and of self-instruction. In a sense, it would need to revive the project for a 'Library of the Best Foreign Socialist Writers' that Marx, Engels and Moses Hess proposed to a German publisher in 1845, but which never came to fruition. Among the authors whom Marx, Engels and Hess thought worthy of translation, appeared the following names: Mably, Morelly, Godwin, Fourier, Owen, Buonarroti. By referring to *The German Ideology*, we can also add: Thomas More, the Levellers . . . Thompson, Watts, Holyoake, Harney, Morgan, Southwell, Goodwyn Barmby, Greaves, Edmonds, Hobson, Spence . . .[43] In addition, one should not forget Cabet, Lamennais and others.

In order not merely to satisfy one's literary curiosity, but rather to provide documentation on the precursors of Marx's activity as a militant theorist, it would also be appropriate to recall the works which he and Engels, as supposedly 'scientific' socialists, had amassed in their personal libraries. It is known that in 1849, before Marx left the Continent for London, he possessed a well-equipped library. Among the authors whose works he is known to have collected, we can pick out the following (while omitting numerous others whose works in the fields of political economy, the history of revolutions, and classical and modern philosophy he is also known to have possessed):

> Louis Blanc, Eugène Buret, Condorcet, G. de Beaumont, Destutt de Tracy, Dézamy, Adam Ferguson, Feuerbach, Fourier, Godwin, Guizot, Moses Hess, P. H. D. d'Holbach, Hegel, Pierre Leroux, Mably, Montaigne, Montesquieu, Morelly, Owen, Paine, Pecqueur, Proudhon, Louis Reybaud, Rousseau, Wilhelm Schulz, Lorenz Stein, Weitling.[44]

To silence any future legend concerning Marx's would-be 'system of thought', he gave the following characterisation of himself, when writing to his daughter Laura on 11 April 1868:

> You'll certainly fancy, my dear child, that I am very fond of books, because I trouble you with them at so unseasonable a time. [Laura was in Paris on honeymoon with her husband Paul Lafargue.] But you would be quite mistaken. I am a machine condemned to devour them and then, throw them, in a changed form, on the dunghill of history.[45]

Notes

1. Karl Marx and Frederick Engels, *Collected Works*, vol. IV (London: Lawrence & Wishart, 1975) pp. 229ff.
2. Marx and Engels, vol. VI (1976) pp. 507–17.
3. Ibid, p. 508.
4. Ibid, p. 509.
5. Ibid, pp. 509–10.
6. Ibid, p. 509.
7. Marx and Engels, vol. V (1976) pp. 455ff.
8. Ibid, pp. 484–530.
9. Marx and Engels, vol. VI (1976) p. 513.
10. Otto Rühle, *Karl Marx, His Life and Work* (London: George Allen & Unwin, 1929) p. 110.
11. Marx and Engels, vol. VI (1976) pp. 105ff.
12. Ibid, pp. 513–14.
13. See *The Holy Family* (1845), in Marx and Engels, vol. IV (1975) p. 32.
14. Marx and Engels, vol. VI (1976) p. 514.
15. Ibid, p. 515.
16. Marx and Engels, vol. IV (1975) p. 119 (emphases in the original).
17. Marx and Engels, vol. VI (1976) p. 516.
18. Ibid, p. 516.
19. Marx and Engels, Vol. IV (1975) p. 667.
20. Ibid, p. 132.
21. Ibid, p. 131 (emphases in the original).
22. See Marx and Engels, vol. VI (1976) pp. 415ff.
23. This word is deleted in the manuscript.
24. Marx and Engels, vol. VI (1976) p. 576.
25. Marx and Engels, vol. III (1975) p. 402.
26. Ibid, p. 202.
27. Marx and Engels, vol. VI (1976) p. 516.
28. Ibid, p. 495.
29. Maximilien Rubel, 'Marx théoricien de l'anarchisme', in *Les Cahiers du Vent du Ch'min*, 5 (Saint-Denis: 1983).
30. Marx and Engels, vol. VI (1976) p. 515.
31. Karl Marx, *Capital*, vol. I (Chicago: Charles H. Kerr, 1919) p. 836.

32. Ibid, pp. 836–7.
33. Georges Sorel, *Matériaux pour une théorie du prolétariat* (Paris: Marcel Rivière, 1921) p. 189.
34. Ibid, p. 189 (emphases in the original). Sorel wrote the chapter from which this passage is taken in 1899.
35. See Georges Sorel, 'Morale et socialisme', in *Le Mouvement Social*, I (March 1899) pp. 207–13, and 'L'Ethique du socialisme', in *Revue de Métaphysique et de Morale*, VII (May 1899) pp. 280–301.
36. Marx, vol. I (1919) p. 837.
37. Ibid, p. 837.
38. Ibid, p. 837. For the original, see Marx and Engels, vol. VI (1976) p. 496.
39. Marx, vol. I (1919) p. 41.
40. Ibid, pp. 14–15.
41. Karl Kraus, *Sprüche und Widersprüche* (Vienna/Leipzig: 1924) p. 81.
42. E. P. Thompson, *The Making of the English Working Class* (London: Victor Gollancz, 1963) p. 11.
43. *The German Ideology* (1845–6) in Marx and Engels, vol. V (1976) p. 461. See also Engels's letters to Marx dated 22 February–7 March 1845 and 17 March 1845 in Marx and Engels, vol. XXXVIII (1982) pp. 21–30.
44. See *Ex libris Karl Marx und Friedrich Engels. Schicksal und Verzeichnis einer Bibliothek* (Berlin: Dietz Verlag, 1967).
45. Maximilien Rubel and Margaret Manale, *Marx Without Myth* (Oxford: Blackwell, 1975) p. 232.

2 The Thin Red Line: Non-Market Socialism in the Twentieth Century

John Crump

From a socialist standpoint, what is the most crucial difference between the nineteenth century and the twentieth century?

Although one could point to numerous differences which are significant for socialists, surely the most crucial difference of all is that in the nineteenth century there were no states which claimed to be socialist. Despite the well-known distinction which Marx, Engels and others made between 'scientific socialism' and 'utopian socialism', even nineteenth-century 'scientific socialism' was utopian in the etymological sense of referring to nowhere – to no existing state. By way of contrast, for most of the twentieth century, states have existed which have been popularly regarded as 'socialist' or 'communist'. The effect of this popular identification of 'socialism' with certain states has been disastrous. Millions of wage-earners have drawn the conclusion that socialism has been tried in the twentieth century and found to fail. Even many stern critics of the 'socialist states' have been reduced to describing such countries as examples of 'actually existing socialism'.[1] Capitalism has been given a new lease of life because, compared with the brutality of state capitalist regimes or the cynicism of Social Democratic administrations, government by even avowedly capitalist parties has seemed preferable to many.

SOCIAL DEMOCRACY AND LENINISM

During the twentieth century, 'socialism' has come to mean for most people either Social Democracy or Leninism. Social Democracy has been strongest in the countries of Western and Northern Europe, where Social Democratic Parties have held power for varying lengths of time. Most Social Democratic governments have practised a policy of selective nationalisation, bringing key (and often problem-ridden) industries under state control. Implicit in such a policy has been both the preservation of the state, which is obviously strengthened as sectors of the economy are brought under its control, and the preservation of capitalism. Social Democracy has had the effect of preserving capitalism because the Social Democratic 'mixed economy' is a mixture of private capitalism and state capitalism. Private companies in the 'mixed economy' remain profit-making enterprises. Part of their profits is reinvested in production, while the residue is partly consumed by capitalists who own shares in the companies and partly acquired by the state in the form of taxes. The nationalised sectors of the 'mixed economy' conform to this pattern of profit distribution no less than private companies. State enterprises are intended to make profits, although lack of commercial viability has often been a reason for declining industries being nationalised. Where profits are realised by nationalised concerns, there is the same three-way division of the profits as in private industry, between the reinvestment fund, the state, and capitalists who own shares or bonds.

Throughout the 'mixed economy', in private and nationalised concerns alike, goods and services are produced for sale on the market. Production is geared to market requirements rather than to human needs, and distribution of goods and services is handled by buying and selling operations, achieved by the use of money. Similarly, throughout the 'mixed economy', production is undertaken by working men and women who sell their labour power for wages (or salaries). Whether the 'mixed economy' is considered from the viewpoint of consumers, whose level of consumption is determined by the money at their disposal, or from the viewpoint of wage-earners, who must sell their labour power to an enterprise which is prepared to employ them, the differences between the private capitalist and state capitalist sectors of the economy are insignificant.[2]

At its most well-meaning, Social Democracy has represented an attempt to humanise and reform capitalism by means of state intervention. One reason why Social Democrats have failed in their attempts to transform capitalism into a humane system is that invariably they have attempted to carry out their reforms within the narrow confines of a single nation- state, which has necessarily remained an integral part of the world market. In the end, the world market has had a more decisive influence on the production of wealth and the intensity of labour than the however-well-intentioned reforms legislated by Social Democrats. Social Democrats inevitably have been driven to administer capitalism in the only way it can be administered – against the interests of the wage-earning majority. Social Democracy has suffered this fate of continuing to oppress wage-earners not because of the failure of its leaders, because they lacked will and nerve, but because of the very nature of capitalism. Nevertheless, it is fair to say that once most Social Democrats have tasted state power, and have found themselves responding to the dictates of the world market, so their good intentions have rapidly been eroded by political cynicism. The record of Social Democracy in the twentieth century has not only been one of submission to capitalism, but also one of support for wars, apology for privilege and compromise with the spurious democracy of parliamentarism. The result of advocating a 'mixed economy' is that the achievement of 'socialism' has been endlessly postponed. The Social Democrats' 'socialism' continually has receded into the future, in a similar fashion, as we shall see, to the 'communism' of the Leninists.

In contrast to Social Democracy, most of the countries where Leninist Parties have taken power have been located in Eastern Europe and East Asia. The different geographical locations of Social Democracy and Leninism reflect the fact that these two political movements have developed in response to the needs of countries at different stages of economic development. Whereas Social Democracy has made little headway in other than advanced countries, Leninism has largely been confined to backward countries. Except in the case of certain East European countries, where the imposition of the Leninist political model has resulted from the extension of Russian military influence, Leninist Parties have generally captured power against a backcloth of revolutionary upheaval arising from the failure of the pre-revolutionary regimes to achieve sustained economic growth and industrialisation.

Following the revolutionary seizure of power, Leninism proceeds with an attempt to achieve forced economic development by means of restricting workers' and peasants' consumption in the interest of rapid capital accumulation. Under these circumstances, in Leninist vocabulary, 'socialism' means a policy of generalised nationalisation (at least within the industrial sectors of the economy) and a vast increase in wage labour, since newly created enterprises require fresh drafts of wage-earners to operate them. The strengthening of the state by virtue of its role as the general employer, and the extension of wage labour, clearly contradict the nineteenth-century socialist prescriptions that the state should wither away and that the wages system should be abolished. Leninism has 'solved' this problem ideologically by relegating the withering-away of the state and the abolition of wages to a continually receding 'communist' future. Meanwhile, the term 'socialism' is retained as a descriptive label for a situation where the state has unparalleled power and where workers have no alternative but to work for wages in order to gain the means of life. In other words, Leninism uses a 'socialist' label to hide the real nature of an economy which differs from private capitalism only in the fact that the state has replaced the privately owning capitalist class as the owner of the means of production. Since the countries where Leninist Parties hold power exhibit all the key features of capitalism (production for profit, monetary distribution, wage labour, accumulation of capital) and are forced to attune their production in line with international competition as it registers on the world market, they are best understood as state capitalist countries.[3]

If state capitalism expresses the *economic* reality of Leninism, *politically* the hallmark of Leninism is the extreme concentration of power. No political formation is tolerated outside the umbrella of the ruling triumvirate, made up of the party, the state and the armed forces. The vanguard party operates in the name of the working class but in fact looks after the interests of the *de facto* state capitalist class, which is composed of the upper echelons of the party, state and military hierarchies. Nationalism and militarism are other important ingredients in the political cocktail of Leninism, and the prominent role which they play reflects the economic backwardness of most countries where Leninist Parties have taken power. In the cut-throat world of capitalist competition, economic backwardness is generally accompanied by subordination to imperialism, so that revolutions aimed at developing a backward country on a state capitalist basis are also expressions of national independence. Hence, flying in the face of the socialist common sense of the nineteenth century that 'the working men have no country',[4] Leninist Parties that have come to power have attempted to hitch the working class to the chariot of military defence of national interests.

For the reasons outlined above, our contention is that Social Democracy and Leninism are bankrupt insofar as the interests of the wage-earning working class are concerned. Anyone who has preserved the critical consciousness of nineteenth-century non-market socialism can see that, in the twentieth century, Social Democracy and Leninism have bolstered, rather than subverted, capitalism. The bankruptcy of Social Democracy and Leninism should be particularly clear in the light of the present economic crisis. The crisis has arisen because the chaotic nature of capitalism has led to capital's inability to realise sufficient profit in production, and hence to a contracting world market. It has been a worldwide crisis, affecting private capitalist, 'mixed economy' and state capitalist countries alike. Social Democracy and Leninism have been unable to offer any credible solutions to the crisis (and are unable to solve the hardships which capitalism imposes on wage-earners even outside of crisis situations) because the alternatives to private capitalism which they represent are no more than alternative methods of organising capitalism. They have no alternative to production for the world market, even though it is the world market which has produced the crisis.

THE THIN RED LINE

To find a coherent set of ideas which are subversive of capitalism, and which do offer an alternative to production for the world market, one must turn to the 'thin red line' represented by the five currents which are examined in the following chapters. In roughly chronological order of appearance, these five currents are: anarcho-communism; impossibilism; council communism; Bordigism; situationism. A thorough consideration of each current will be left until the relevant chapter, but there are brief profiles of these currents in the Introduction for the benefit of readers who may be unfamiliar with them.

Even a perfunctory acquaintance with the five currents which jointly represent the 'thin red line' of non-market socialism in the twentieth century leads to the realisation that their importance does not lie in the number of their adherents, or in their influence on the course of world history. Although some of these currents have enjoyed moments of transitory glory/notoriety, throughout most of the twentieth century it has been possible to discount them in terms of the support which they have attracted and their impact on the world. The question therefore arises: if the significance of the non-market socialists does not lie in their numbers and influence, where does it lie? The answer is that non-market socialism is significant because its various currents represent successful attempts by groups of working men and women to formulate a fundamental critique of capitalism and simultaneously to pose a genuinely socialist alternative. Considered in isolation, it is easy to dismiss any one of the five currents as too small and too uninfluential to be important. Taken together, however, they represent a sustained response on the part of wage labour to capitalist exploitation and irrationality. Irrespective of the limited numbers of wage-earners involved, non-market socialism should be seen as an authentic response to capitalism by wage labour because, as the existence of the various non-market socialist currents demonstrates, groups of wage-earners have repeatedly, and largely independently of one another, formulated the same critique of capitalism and the same alternative of socialism. The fact that this has occurred at different historical junctures, and in different geographical and cultural contexts, gives weight to the claim that, as long as world capitalism persists, groups of wage-earning men and women are certain to emerge who will challenge capital's priority of production for the market and call on their fellow-workers to take joint action in order to establish the human community of socialism.

It is important to emphasise the scale of the claim which is being made here with regard to non-market socialism. It is not being suggested that non-market socialism is another socialist tradition which should be placed alongside Social Democracy and Leninism, and seen as a rival to them. The claim is considerably more audacious than that. What is being argued is that, collectively, anarcho-communism, impossibilism, council communism, Bordigism and situationism *are* socialism in the twentieth century. Outside these currents, socialism has not existed, since what conventionally are considered to be the great victories of 'socialism' in the twentieth century have been nothing more than extensions of state capitalism at the expense of private capitalism. Social Democracy and Leninism have made priceless contributions to world capitalism by deflecting working-class criticism away from the key elements of capitalism as a mode of production to the contingent, and increasingly obsolete, manifestations of capitalism in its private capitalist form. Only those working men and women who have looked at capitalism from the perspective provided by non-market socialism have been able to see through capitalism in all its forms and have avoided capitulation to one side or another in struggles between rival capitalist interests.

Implicit in this argument is a criticism of the conventional method of political analysis, which seeks to understand the world in terms of a 'left'/'right' dichotomy. The 'left' and the 'right' are different only to the extent that they provide a different political and organisational apparatus for administering the same capitalist system. What the 'left' and the 'right' have in common is that they both accept the world market as the framework in which they must operate. Since both the 'left' and the 'right' stand for the perpetuation of wage labour, it follows that they cannot offer convincing solutions to the problems which inevitably confront wage-earners. A permanent solution to the problems which are inherent in wage labour, such as insecurity and intensity of work, can only lie in the abolition of the wages system. Yet the abolition of the wages system is a demand which cannot be located on the 'left'–'right' political spectrum. Only the various currents which represent non-market socialism have consistently demanded an end to wage labour, and that is why they too cannot usefully be identified in terms of a 'left'/'right' orientation.

THE PRINCIPLES OF SOCIALISM

In order to sustain the claim that, collectively, anarcho-communism, impossibilism, council communism, Bordigism and situationism are twentieth-century socialism, it needs to demonstrated that there is a basic set of socialist principles which these currents share. Initially, four such principles can be identified. The currents of non-market socialism are all committed to establishing a new society where:

(1) Production will be for use, and not for sale on the market.
(2) Distribution will be according to need, and not by means of buying and selling.
(3) Labour will be voluntary, and not imposed on workers by means of a coercive wages system.
(4) A human community will exist, and social divisions based on class, nationality, sex or race will have disappeared.

Let us clarify these four principles for those readers who may not immediately grasp all their ramifications.

1. Production for Use

The means of production will be owned and controlled communally, and will be used to produce whatever men, women and children need to enjoy full and satisfying lives. Levels of production will be determined by people's freely expressed desires – that is, their desires for articles of individual and social consumption and their desires to engage in creative work. Communal ownership means that all people will freely have access to the means of production, and that no section of the population will be able to exclude others from using the means of production or from enjoying the fruits of production. Production will be coordinated at local, regional and global levels, and communal control means that all people will again be free to participate in managing production and administering society as a whole. Just as no individual or group will be able to prevent others from engaging in direct production, so no section of the population will be able to exclude others from the management of production or from the administration of society.

The details of what to produce and how to produce will be decided locally. The responsibilities of the regional and global bodies will be threefold. In the first place, they will provide the statistical services which will allow production to be coordinated. Second, they will ensure that products which localities need but cannot produce are available to those localities. Third, they will handle the movement of local products at the regional and global levels. By confining the functions of regional and global bodies to these activities, they will not assume the role which the state fulfils in class-divided societies. They will not be provided with armed forces, and therefore will not be in a position to impose decisions on others.

All this is in evident contrast to capitalism. Like any mode of production, capitalism is provided with a mechanism for coordinating production. In capitalism's case, this mechanism is the market. But the price inherent in relying on the market is that levels of production are determined not by people's social or even biological needs, but by the population's 'effective demand' expressed as buying power. The needs of those without the ability to pay do not register on the market, and this results in means of production lying idle while millions of people are deprived. Such a barbaric situation would be impossible in the society envisaged by non-market socialists.

2. Distribution According to Need

People will be free to take whatever they choose from the consumption outlets ('shops without cash registers') in the new society, without making any payment, since money will not exist. Similarly, people will freely make use of social facilities, such as theatres and libraries, without entering into exchange relationships (i.e. buying tickets or paying fees). Non-market socialists are confident that society could run smoothly on this basis, without being undermined by people becoming insatiably greedy or indulging in recklessly extravagant consumption. Our confidence derives from a number of considerations. First, the production of useful articles would be much greater in the new society than in capitalism, not only because production would be freed from the constraints of the market, but also because all those presently engaged in activities which are specific to a commercial society (banking, insurance and so on), or in activities which are specific to a class-divided society (such as staffing the numerous arms of the repressive apparatus of the state), could redirect their efforts towards production. Second, since greed and conspicuous consumption are reactions to scarcity, we can expect these forms of behaviour to disappear in a society which raises production to the level where it guarantees everyone an abundant supply of all that is required for a comfortable and satisfying life. Third, in a society which is based on cooperation rather than competition, not only would the individual's sense of solidarity induce him or her to exercise self-control on occasions when this was necessary, but social disapproval would be a powerful restraint on any who were disposed to reckless extravagance.

3. Voluntary Labour

In the new society, everyone will have the right to consume, irrespective of whether they are engaged in productive activity or not. Nevertheless, non-market socialists anticipate that people will volunteer to work, and will freely give their time and effort to ensure that an abundant supply of products is constantly available. To those whose horizons do not extend beyond capitalist society, these expectations must seem preposterous. Under capitalism, workers are coerced into engaging in production by the system which makes their consumption dependent on their wages. Work within capitalism therefore is conflated with employment, and popularly is regarded merely as a means to leisure (= consumption), which becomes the end to which life is supposed to be directed.

However, non-market socialists argue that once work and employment are conceptually distinguished, work can be seen as an activity which is not merely enjoyable, but which it is biologically necessary for human beings to engage in (on a par with eating, drinking, breathing and sex). Freed from its alienating form of wage labour, work will become a creative and rewarding experience which it would be painful for people to deprive themselves of. The boring and monotonous toil of capitalism will be replaced by stimulating and diversified patterns of work, and many of the dangerous occupations which are found within capitalism will be eliminated. Capitalism has already made these changes technically possible, but is prevented from realising them because considerations of profit outweigh human welfare. Any dangerous work which remains in the new society will be undertaken voluntarily and the only reward for the men and women engaged in it will be society's affection and esteem (as with lifeboat crews and mountain rescue teams, for example, even under capitalism).

4. A Human Community

Capitalism is a divided society. The basic divisions within capitalism are class divisions, which exist because the means of production are owned and controlled by sections of the population and not by society as a whole. Sectional ownership can be maintained only when it is constantly reinforced by the state, and since states exercise their authority over geographical areas, national divisions are perpetuated by capitalism. Furthermore, since labour power is a marketable commodity under capitalism, wage-earners throughout the world compete with one another to sell their labour power to those who employ them. Such competition forms the basis of the sexual, racial and other divisions which divide the working class, and which are skilfully manipulated by the ruling class in order to maintain capital's ascendancy over wage labour.

The society envisaged by non-market socialists would remove all these divisions at one stroke, by realising the communal ownership of the means of production. Since capitalism is an integrated economic system whose market encompasses the whole world, it can be removed only by an equally world-enveloping system which displaces the market. The new society which non-market socialists envisage must therefore be a human community on a global scale. National frontiers will not exist. Cultural and linguistic diversity might flourish within the human community of socialism, but in a moneyless world where distribution was according to need, there would be no way in which the embracing of a certain culture or the use of a certain language could confer economic advantages or disadvantages. In a world owned by all, all would be brothers and sisters.

Although these four basic socialist principles are shared by the currents which represent non-market socialism, they are not sufficient for distinguishing the non-market socialists from all their political opponents. We said before that 'communism' figures in Leninist ideology as a mirage which is forever receding into the distance, and this enables Leninists of all hues to subscribe *in the long term* to these four basic socialist principles. For example, books published with the approval of the Russian state inform us that:

> Under communism, consumer goods – to say nothing of capital goods [*sic*] – cease to be commodities. Trade and money will outlive themselves. Flats, cultural, communication and transport facilities, meals, laundries, clothes, etc., will all be free.
>
> Stores and shops will be turned into public warehouses where members of communist society will be supplied with commodities [*sic*] for personal use. The need for wages and other forms of remuneration will disappear.[5]

Apart from the silly slips about capital and commodities existing in communism, this could be taken as an acceptable sketch of the new society. Even better – since he drops Lenin's arbitrary distinction between 'socialism' and 'communism' – is what the Trotskyist Ernest Mandel has written about a 'socialist economy':

> The withering-away of commodity and money economy is, however, only one of the factors bringing about the disappearance of social inequality, classes and the state.[6]

A fifth principle is therefore required in order to distinguish the non-market socialists from all varieties of Leninists, including the Trotskyists. This principle can be formulated as follows:

(5) Opposition to capitalism as it manifests itself in *all* existing countries.

Non-market socialists do not take sides in the wars and struggles for supremacy between rival states which are a permanent feature of world capitalism. On the contrary, non-market socialists are hostile to all states, including those which falsely proclaim themselves as 'socialist' or 'workers' states'. Indeed, it was the various currents of non-market socialists who pioneered the theory of state capitalism in order to clarify the nature of self-styled 'workers' states', starting with Russia, and in order to give a theoretical explanation for their refusal to support such states.

STATE CAPITALISM

Following the Russian Revolution of 1917, the US government deported a number of activists who were of Russian origin, including the anarcho-communists Alexander Berkman and Emma Goldman. Berkman and Goldman went to Russia and observed Leninist rule at first hand. On the basis of his experiences, Berkman described the Russian economy in 1922 as 'a combination of State and private capitalism'[7] and this view was echoed by anarcho-communists elsewhere. As Ōsugi Sakae wrote in Japan, also in 1922: 'the struggle between the proletariat on one side and state and private capitalism on the other is still continuing in Russia'.[8]

The council communist Otto Rühle journeyed to Russia in 1920 and reported in 1921, after his return to Germany, that: 'The dictatorship of the party is commissar-despotism, is state capitalism.'[9] A decade later, various council communist groups issued in Holland a set of *Theses on Bolshevism*, which declared in part:

> The socialization concept of the Bolsheviks is therefore nothing but a capitalist economy taken over by the State and directed from the outside and above by its bureaucracy. The Bolshevik socialism is state-organized capitalism.[10]

Despite the fact that no members of the impossibilist Socialist Party of Great Britain (SPGB) visited Russia in the immediate aftermath of the 1917 Revolution, by 1920 from its vantage point in Britain, the *Socialist Standard* was already able to discern that Leninist policy amounted to state capitalism.[11] At a later stage, when Lenin was dead and his successors were engaged in a vicious struggle for power, the SPGB clearly expressed the non-market socialist conviction that, since Leninists of all types are advocates of capitalism, from a working-class standpoint there is nothing to choose between them. Commenting on the struggle between Stalin and Trotsky, the *Socialist Standard* wrote: 'Both Trotsky and Stalin draw up their programmes within the framework of state and private capitalism which prevails in Russia.'[12]

Although the Bordigists and the situationists reached the conclusion that state capitalism exists in Russia and elsewhere at a later stage than the other currents of non-market socialists, for many years now all five currents have attempted to dispel popular illusions about the state capitalist countries. Not only have they exposed the capitalist features of the state capitalist countries, but they have counterposed to state capitalism the alternative vision of a genuinely socialist society which could liberate humankind from indignity and oppression by incorporating principles 1–4 which we outlined above. It is this, above all, which distinguishes the non-market socialists from the Trotskyists and other varieties of Leninists. The Trotskyists have been inhibited from counterposing to capitalism the alternative of non-market socialism, because the focus of their attention has been the relatively minor differences which exist between traditional, private capitalism and capitalism as it manifests itself in their so-called 'workers' states'. To express this schematically, the Trotskyists' failure to embrace principle 5 has caused principles 1–4 to be relegated to (at best) the background of their concerns. Alternatively, one could say that the Trotskyists have lost their 'utopianism' (i.e. their identification with no nation-state) by allowing themselves to be sucked into struggles between rival capitals and by electing to defend some capitalist states against others. This has resulted in an unbridgeable divide between Trotskyism and the five currents of non-market socialism.

DIFFERENCES BETWEEN THE NON-MARKET SOCIALISTS

Having identified the five principles which the various currents of non-market socialists collectively hold, the issues which have separated these currents and provoked their mutual criticism must also be considered briefly.

The anarcho-communists have seen Marxism as yet another

form of politics which seeks to maintain the power of the state. Not only have anarcho-communists identified Marxism with statism in general, but in particular they have identified Marxism with the Leninist states. They have argued that the characteristics of Leninist state capitalism derive from the Marxist principles on which it claims to be based. Conversely, just as the anarcho-communists generally have made no distinction between Marxism and Leninism, so the other non-market socialist currents have reciprocated by indiscriminately lumping the anarcho-communists together with all other varieties of anarchists, be they Stirnerite individualists, anarcho-capitalist 'libertarians' or whatever. In other words, they have chosen to ignore the commitment of the anarcho-communists to communism.

Although not all impossibilists have been committed to parliamentary activity, the SPGB – as the best-known impossibilist group – has been separated from the other currents of non-market socialists perhaps above all by its belief that parliamentary elections can be put to a revolutionary use. The SPGB has insisted that the paradigm of socialist revolution consists of the working class consciously electing a majority of socialist MPs to the national assemblies in different countries, whereupon 'the machinery of government . . . may be converted from an instrument of oppression into the agent of emancipation'.[13] A parliamentary strategy of this type has been anathema to the other currents of non-market socialists.

Council communism has emphasised the part to be played by councils in the projected socialist revolution, and has combined its advocacy of councils with hostility towards trade unions. One repercussion of this emphasis on councils has been a perennial difficulty faced by council communists when it comes to deciding the respective roles of the workers' councils and the political party. Hence, one can say that not only has the council communists' emphasis on councils separated them from the other currents of non-market socialists, but that it has also acted as a source of division among the council communists themselves. In extreme cases, attachment to the workers' councils as an organisational form has entirely eclipsed the communist element in council communism, resulting in a variety of 'councillism' which is compatible with production for the market.

The Bordigists have seen themselves as a vanguard which must lead the working class to socialism. Their conviction that they have the responsibility to lead the working class derives from the premise that only after the achievement of socialism could the mass of the workers become conscious socialists. The other currents of non-market socialists have denounced the Bordigists' vanguardism and have argued that (to quote from the statutes of the First International) 'the emancipation of the working class must be the act of the working class itself'[14] and not of self-appointed leaders.

Perhaps because of their artistic origins, the situationists have often seemed to be more concerned with self-expression than with communicating their ideas to wage-earners. The situationists have seen the other currents of non-market socialists as outdated and, at best, the products of earlier stages of capitalist development. On the other hand, the other currents of non-market socialists have often criticised the situationists as 'modernists' who have been overly influenced by current intellectual fashions and who have shirked the arduous toil of sustained, organised activity within the working class.

The differences between the various currents of non-market socialists are deep-rooted and have acted to keep these currents separate from one another and mutually hostile. Despite this, the claim which is advanced here is that these differences constitute a 'periphery' which is relatively less important than the commonly held 'core' of socialist principles which were examined earlier. What grounds are there for regarding the 'core' as more significant than the 'periphery'? Essentially, the argument is that the 'core' principles of socialism relate to the vital task of posing a socialist alternative to capitalism, while the 'peripheral' differences largely arise from the debate over how socialism can be achieved (by means of parliamentary elections, workers' councils, vanguard parties and so on). Of course, one cannot pretend that the method of achieving socialism is an unimportant question. Certainly, the choice of means has implications for the nature of the projected end. Nevertheless, in the circumstances of the twentieth century, when socialism is widely misunderstood as Social Democracy and Leninism, the prime responsibility of socialists is to encourage wage-earners, as they come into conflict with capital, to see that a non-market alternative to capitalist production represents the only lasting solution to their problems. In this regard, all five currents of non-market socialists have played a positive role. On the other hand, precisely because for most of this century mere handfuls of wage-earners have been committed to non-market socialism, the fierce polemics over the means to achieve socialism which non-market socialists have engaged in have been largely academic.

One can illustrate the above argument by taking the Bordigists as an example and considering further their commitment to vanguardism. As has already been mentioned, with the exception of the Bordigists, most non-market socialists reject the idea that a vanguard can lead the wage-earners to socialism. They interpret the maxim of the First International that 'the emancipation of the working class must be the act of the working class itself' to mean that capitalism can only be overthrown, and that socialism can only be achieved, by a majority of conscious socialists. On the other hand, the Bordigists believe that a socialist majority is unattainable under capitalism. They envisage the socialist revolution in terms of action by a vanguard because they insist that only in the changed material conditions of socialism could the majority become socialists.

Some non-market socialists would see this as sufficient reason for denying that the Bordigists are socialists. However, I think it can be shown that the Bordigists' vanguardism is not crucially important in the present situation. Like the other currents of non-market socialists, the Bordigists engage in activity to challenge capitalist ideology and to popularise socialist ideas. Depending on the country and the cultural environment in which they exist, wage-earners may stumble across the Bordigists or across one of the other currents of non-market socialism. Just as with any other current of non-market socialism, wage-earners who make contact with the Bordigists will find the experience useful for gaining a recognition of what socialism genuinely means. Similarly, they can gain from the Bordigists an understanding that capitalism is a single, unified world system, which exists in all countries and dominates the entire globe. Looked at in this way, the question of vanguardism has little significance *under present circumstances*. Any wage-earner who encounters the Bordigists and is impressed by their theories is accepted as part of the vanguard. Nobody who agrees is turned away; it is assumed that they are part of the vanguard.

The Bordigists' image of themselves as a vanguard is not vitally important at present because the question of vanguardism will ultimately be settled by the practical actions of wage-earners at the relevant time. It is up to the wage-earners to carry out the socialist revolution and to prove the Bordigists wrong. Of course, if the Bordigists persisted with their determination to act as a vanguard even in the face of a majority of conscious socialists, the situation would be drastically different from that which currently pertains – and this would call for a drastically different response. Suppose that under the circumstances where a majority of conscious socialists were actually engaged in transforming society to socialism, the Bordigists were to proclaim: 'Hands off the socialist revolution! It is our affair. We do not recognise that you workers are capable of achieving socialist consciousness.' Clearly, in such a situation, additional principles to those which have been formulated to cover *present* circumstances would swiftly be generated, and equally swiftly (and deservedly) the workers would sweep the Bordigists and all other would-be leaders aside.

Implicit in the foregoing discussion is the idea that the distinction between 'core' and 'periphery' is not fixed, but reflects the prevailing circumstances. In the current situation, the prime responsibility of socialists is to challenge the economic mechanism and the set of social relations which constitute capitalism by demonstrating that society would be organised differently in socialism. The core principles of socialism which were formulated earlier are a reflection of this priority, in that they are principally concerned with the question of (capitalist or socialist) ends. In a different situation, when the socialist revolution was imminent, the question of means (how to effect the socialist transformation of society) would also demand urgent attention. Consequently, the key principles of socialism would necessarily have to be extended in order to encompass the pressing questions of means as well as ends. As a result, the boundary between 'core' and 'peripheral' questions would naturally alter, and a more extensive set of criteria for distinguishing socialists from non-socialists would be required than at present. However, to anticipate this development, and to construct artificially an extended set of socialist principles which encompass means as well as ends, even when the circumstances of the socialist revolution lie in the future and hence are speculative, is to ignore material conditions and to construct a suprahistorical theory.

One reason why the distinction between 'core' and 'peripheral' areas of their theory has not been made by the non-market socialists is the tendency of most currents to set themselves up as a minuscule group or 'party', which boasts a detailed programme encompassing every aspect of socialist theory. Under current conditions, the group then becomes a besieged citadel which confronts not only the hostile capitalist world but also the majority of wage-earners, whose ideas about socialism are the result of the illusions spread by Social Democrats and Leninists. In such a situation, the group battles to maintain its doctrinal purity in the face of the constant threat of being swamped by the ideology of capitalism. The very survival of the group seems to depend on the grim defence of every dot and comma of group doctrine, and the resulting 'besieged citadel' mentality makes it difficult to distinguish what is crucial in the group's programme from what is contingent (in the terms of this discussion, the 'core' from the 'periphery').

REJECTION OF THE 'TRANSITIONAL SOCIETY'

If and when the time comes when the mass of wage-earners turn to non-market socialism as the means to liberate themselves, it is possible, and even likely, that all the existing currents of non-market socialists will be superseded and that an entirely new movement will be built. Even so, the 'core' principles of socialism which the five currents of non-market socialists have collectively maintained will be the theoretical foundation stones on which a mass movement of genuine socialists will be constructed. In fact, the process of superseding the five currents does not lie entirely in the future. It is a process which proceeds continually, so that in recent decades new developments have taken place and groups have emerged which are significant.

In my view, the most important development which needs to take place within the milieu of non-market socialism (and which, to an extent, is taking place) is for the notion of a supposed 'transitional society' between capitalism and socialism to be rejected. To the extent that this development occurs, it enables non-market socialism to differentiate itself even more clearly from Social Democracy and Leninism, by adding a further principle to the five socialist principles which we identified earlier. The sixth principle can be formulated as follows:

(6) Capitalism can be transcended only by immediately being replaced by socialism.

To talk in terms of capitalism 'immediately being replaced by socialism' is not to suggest that socialism will be free of problems when it is first established. No doubt, the mess which capitalism has made of the world will ensure that there are major problems which a newly emergent socialist society will have to solve. Yet what the phrase 'immediately being replaced by socialism' does imply is that the solution of these problems bequeathed by capitalism will have to take place from the outset on a socialist basis. Various approaches which are popularly misunderstood as 'transitional' can be ruled out in advance. For example, one could not have bits of socialism transplanted into still-functioning capitalism, any more than elements of capitalism could be left *in situ* within newly established socialism. Still less could one legitimately describe the doomed offspring which would result from such far-fetched attempts at social hybridisation as a 'transitional society'.

One feature which capitalism and socialism have in common is their all-or-nothing quality, their inability to coexist in today's highly integrated world, which can provide an environment for only one or other of these rival global systems. In the circumstances of the twentieth century, the means of production must either function as capital throughout the world (in which case wage labour and capitalism persist internationally) or they must be commonly owned and democratically controlled at a global level (in which case they would be used to produce wealth for free, worldwide distribution). No half-way house between these two starkly opposed alternatives exists, and it is the impossibility of discovering any viable 'transitional' structures which ensures that the changeover from world capitalism to world socialism will have to take the form of a short, sharp rupture (a revolution), rather than an extended process of cumulative transformation.

How, then, might a newly emergent socialist society solve problems, such as shortage of food, which capitalism has created? The first point to make is that the problem of twentieth-century hunger is a social problem and not a technical problem. Technically, the means to feed the world's population are within humankind's reach, but it is capitalism's priority of production for profit which prevents plentiful conditions from being actually realised. Socialism will remove the straitjacket which calculations of profitability impose on production, so that a situation of abundance – where men, women and children throughout the world will be able to take according to their self-determined needs – will be rapidly achieved.

Nevertheless, accessible though such a situation is, its achievement will require time. The time involved will certainly be nothing like the relatively lengthy process which Marx envisaged in 1875 before 'all the springs of co-operative wealth flow more abundantly'.[15] Nothing is more ridiculous today than to repeat the stale formulae of more than one hundred years ago, and hence to ignore the immense developments in the techniques of producing wealth which capitalism has (or, more accurately, the wage-earning wealth producers within capitalism have) brought about. As far as the production of food is concerned, we are talking of at most a few harvests before enough food – and more than enough – could be produced for every man, woman and child to have free access to whatever they required. How might socialist society organise itself during the intervening months or, at most, few years before actual plenty would be produced?

Certainly the answer is not by constructing a 'transitional society' sandwiched between capitalism and socialism. What will be required will be temporary measures which are compatible with, and will lend strength to, emergent socialism; not the construction of a so-called 'transitional society' which would need to be dismantled before socialism could even be instituted. Obviously, the men and women who have newly established socialism will first turn to the 'milk lakes' and the 'butter mountains' which capitalism has accumulated because of its inability to sell such commodities profitably on the world markets. Many nation-states also have strategic stocks of vital supplies, designed to provide some security against the disruption of supplies in the event of war. Since the establishment of socialism will entail the immediate abolition of all markets, nations and wars, sources of supply such as these will be turned to socially useful ends and made freely available.

The scale of any shortages which could not be eliminated by such stop-gap measures is a matter of speculation, but let us assume that shortages would exist for a time before production on a socialist basis could get fully under way and abundance could be attained. How would socialist men and women handle such shortages? It is out of the question that they would make selective use of the wages system or monetary distribution. Such measures would not be 'transitional' but would instead guarantee the continuation of capitalism. Equally unthinkable would be any suggestion that a machinery of state might be retained temporarily as a 'transitional' apparatus for enforcing a rationing system. The persistence of the state would signify that class divisions had not been eradicated. Newly emergent socialism, struggling to solve the problems which it has inherited from capitalism, will have to meet any shortages by relying on the very item it can safely be assumed it will have in abundance: revolutionary enthusiasm.

In the *Critique of the Gotha Programme*, Marx asserted that 'Right can never be higher than the economic structure of society and its cultural development conditioned thereby.'[16] With regard to the long-term functioning of socialist society, he was absolutely right. Any attempt to run socialism, year after year, by compensating for material shortages by ideological appeals to revolutionary enthusiasm would be bound to fail. But thanks to the material advances brought about by capitalism, long-term shortages are not the problems with which socialism would now have to grapple. The problems which are likely to arise are those associated with temporary shortfalls prior to the attainment of abundance; and it is precisely such a transient situation which could be negotiated by relying on revolutionary solidarity.

It will be the revolutionary enthusiasm of millions of socialist men and women, and their determination to make a success of the new society, which will bring about the transformation of the capitalist world in the first place, as they take whatever actions are necessary to bring the means of production under common ownership. These same qualities of enthusiasm and determination will not suddenly evaporate as soon as the means of production are freed from their role of capital. They will exist as a massive reservoir of popular commitment to the goals of socialism, and it is these reserves of revolutionary ardour which people will be able to tap in order to tide society over any period of temporary scarcity. It will be no great hardship for revolutionary men and women to restrict voluntarily certain areas of their own consumption until universal plenty is secured. Having recently stormed the citadels of capitalist power, these selfsame revolutionary men and women will make light of any further period of temporary and selective self-restraint that is necessary – perceiving it as a continuation of the revolution, a small additional price to pay in order to eliminate capitalist misery and indignity for ever.

It always was an illusion to imagine that the route from capitalist scarcity to socialist abundance lies along a diversionary path marked with signposts to an imaginary 'transitional society'. The route to socialism has to be direct; as a moneyless, classless, stateless world community, socialism has to be achieved immediately, or not at all; and any temporary lack of abundance has to be compensated for by the revolutionary enthusiasm of the millions of men and women who will be the collective builders of the socialist world. Fortunately, it is the technological advances of capitalism which have ensured that – given the will for socialism – full-scale abundance can be instituted rapidly. In the light of the productive potential now available to humankind, the notion of a 'transitional society' should clearly be seen not as a bridge leading beyond capitalism, but rather as an ideological barrier obstructing the path to socialism.

The idea of a society which acts as a 'transitional' stage between capitalism and socialism has largely been absent from the thinking of the anarcho-communists, impossibilists and situationists, but it has been entertained by some council communists and the Bordigists. For example, in 1930 the Group of International Communists of Holland (GIC) borrowed some of Marx's speculations in the *Critique of the Gotha Programme* and envisaged a 'transitional society' based on exchange and labour-time calculation.[17] As for the Bordigists, they have taken the view that the party should exercise power after the revolution and administer a society which essentially would remain capitalist for a period until socialism could be achieved. We have seen the dire effects which result from the Trotskyist belief that Russia, China and the other state capitalist countries are 'transitional' 'workers' states'. Council communist and Bordigist ideas have been less damaging because, unlike the Trotskyists, these currents do not identify their notional 'transitional society' with any existing state. Yet, even so, all notions of a 'transitional society' are both mistaken and fraught with peril. They are mistaken because capitalism and socialism (as market and non-market societies respectively) are totally incompatible, so that no 'transitional' combination of capitalist and socialist elements is possible. They are perilous because entertaining the notion of a 'transitional society' inevitably results in the goal of socialism, to a greater or lesser extent, being eclipsed. It is for these reasons that I have argued that all non-market socialists should reject the notion that a 'transitional society' will be interposed between capitalism and socialism. The problems confronting humankind are too grim to allow the wage-earners of the world to solve them by 'transitional' half measures. Only the complete abolition of the market, classes, the state and national frontiers offers hope for the future.

Notes

1. Rudolph Bahro, *The Alternative in Eastern Europe* (London: New Left Books, 1978).
2. Adam Buick and John Crump, *State Capitalism: the Wages System under New Management* (London: Macmillan, 1986).
3. Ibid.

4. Karl Marx and Frederick Engels, *Collected Works*, vol. VI (London: Lawrence & Wishart, 1976) p. 502.
5. *Man's Dreams Are Coming True* (Moscow: Progress, 1966) p. 224.
6. Ernest Mandel, *Marxist Economic Theory* (London: Merlin, 1968) p. 673.
7. Alexander Berkman, *The Russian Tragedy* (Sanday: Cienfuegos, 1976) p. 25.
8. Ōsugi Sakae, 'Rōnō Roshia no Shin Rōdō Undō', in *Ōsugi Sakae Zenshū*, vol. II (Tokyo: 1963) p. 604.
9. Otto Rühle, *From the Bourgeois to the Proletarian Revolution* (London and Glasgow: Socialist Reproduction/Revolutionary Perspectives, 1974) p. xvii.
10. *The Bourgeois Role of Bolshevism* (Glasgow: Glasgow People's Press, no date) p. 21.
11. *Socialist Standard*, July 1920.
12. *Socialist Standard*, December 1928.
13. SPGB, *Declaration of Principles* (1904).
14. David Fernbach, *Karl Marx: the Revolutions of 1848 – Political Writings*, vol. I (Harmondsworth: Penguin, 1973) p. 65.
15. Karl Marx and Frederick Engels, *Selected Works*, vol. III (Moscow: Progress, 1970) p. 19.
16. Ibid, p. 19.
17. 'Temps de travail social moyen: base d'une production et d'une répartition communiste', Supplement to *Informations Correspondances Ouvrières*, 101 (1971); see also Anton Pannekoek, *Workers' Councils* (Cambridge, Mass.: Root and Branch, 1970). For a critical examination of this area of Marx's thought, see John Crump, *A Contribution to the Critique of Marx* (London: Social Revolution/Solidarity, 1975).

3 Anarcho-Communism

Alain Pengam

INTRODUCTION

Anarcho-communism has been regarded by other anarchist currents as a poor and despised relation, an ideological trophy to be exhibited according to the needs of hagiography or polemic before moving on to 'serious things' (the collectivisations in Spain, anarcho-syndicalism, federalism or self-management), and as an 'infantile utopia' more concerned with dogmatic abstractions than with 'economic realities'. Yet anarcho-communism has been the only current within the anarchist movement which has explicitly aimed not only at ending exchange value but, among its most coherent partisans, at making this the immediate content of the revolutionary process. We are speaking here, of course, only of the current which explicitly described itself as 'anarcho-communist', whereas in fact the tendency in the nineteenth century to draw up a stateless communist (but is this not a pleonasm?) 'utopia' extended beyond anarchism properly so-called.

Anarcho-communism must be distinguished from collectivism, which was both a diffuse movement (see, for example, the different components of the International Working Men's Association, the Guesdists and so on) and a specific anarchist current. As far as the latter was concerned, it was Proudhon who supplied its theoretical features: an open opponent of communism (which, for him, was Etienne Cabet's 'communism'), he favoured instead a society in which exchange value would flourish – a society in which workers would be directly and mutually linked to each other by money and the market. The Proudhonist collectivists of the 1860s and 1870s (of whom Bakunin was one), who were resolute partisans of the collective ownership of the instruments of work and, unlike Proudhon, of land, maintained the essence of this commercial structure in the form of groups of producers, organised either on a territorial basis (communes) or on an enterprise basis (cooperatives, craft groupings) and linked to each other by the circulation of value. Collectivism was thus defined – and still is – as an exchange economy where the legal ownership of the instruments of production is held by a network of 'collectivities' which are sorts of workers' joint-stock companies. Most contemporary anarchists (standing, as they do, for a self-managed exchange economy) are collectivists in this nineteenth-century sense of the term, even though the term has now come to have a somewhat different meaning (state ownership, i.e. 'state capitalism', rather than ownership by *any* collectivity).

In the 1870s and 1880s the anarcho-communists, who wanted to abolish exchange value in all its forms, broke with the collectivists, and in so doing revived the tradition of radical communism which had existed in France in the 1840s.

1840–64

In 1843, under the Rabelaisian motto 'Do what you will!', and in opposition to Etienne Cabet, Théodore Dézamy's *Code de la Communauté* laid the basis for the principles developed later in the nineteenth century by communist and anarcho-communist theoreticians such as Joseph Déjacque, Karl Marx, Frederick Engels, William Morris and Peter Kropotkin. These principles involved the abolition of money and commercial exchange; the subordination of the economy to the satisfaction of the needs of the whole population; the abolition of the division of labour (including the division between town and country and between the capital and the provinces); the progressive introduction of attractive work; and the progressive abolition of the state and of the functions of government, as a separate domain of society, following the communisation of social relations, which was to be brought about by a revolutionary government. It should be noted that Dézamy advocated the 'community of goods' and resolutely opposed the specifically collectivist slogan of 'socialisation of property'. In doing so, he anticipated the critical analysis of property which Amadeo Bordiga made more than a century later (see Chapter 6).

Besides rejecting Cabet's utopia, because it maintained the division of labour – in particular that between town and country – and sought to organise it rigidly in the name of economic 'efficiency', Dézamy also refused to insert between the capitalist mode of production and communist society a transitional period of democracy which would have pushed communism into the background. By seeking to establish a direct link between the revolutionary process and the content of communism, so that the dominant class within capitalism would be economically and socially expropriated through the immediate abolition of monetary circulation, Dézamy anticipated what was to be the source of the basic originality of anarcho-communism, in particular in its Kropotkinist form. This feature was the rejection of any 'transition period' that did not encompass the essence of communism: the end of the basic act of buying and selling.

At about the same time, the communists around the journal *L'Humanitaire, organe de la science sociale* (of which two issues appeared in Paris in 1841) advocated a programme of action very close to that of Dézamy,[1] proposing, among other things, the abolition of marriage. In addition, they made travel one of the principal characteristics of communist society, because it would bring about mixing of the races and interchange between industrial and agricultural activities. This group also identified itself with the Babouvist Sylvain Maréchal for having proclaimed 'anti-political and anarchist ideas'.[2] However, it was above all the house-painter Joseph Déjacque (1822–64) who, up until the foundation of anarcho-communism properly so-called, expressed in a coherent way the radical communism which emerged in France from the 1840s as a critical appropriation of Fourierism, Owenism and neo-Babouvism.

Déjacque's work was an examination of the limits of the 1848 revolution and the reasons for its failure. It was developed around a rejection of two things: the state, even if 'revolutionary', and collectivism of the Proudhonist type. Déjacque reformulated communism in a way that sought to be resolutely free from the dogmatism, sectarianism and statism exhibited by those such as Cabet and *La Fraternité de 1845*. Déjacque spoke of: 'Liberty! Which has been so misused against the community and which it is true to say that certain communist schools have held cheap.'[3]

Déjacque was a fierce opponent of all the political gangs of the period. He rejected Blanquism, which was based on a division between the 'disciples of the great people's Architect' and 'the people, or vulgar herd',[4] and was equally opposed to all the variants of social republicanism, to the dictatorship of one man and to 'the dictatorship of the little prodigies of the proletariat'.[5] With regard to the last of these, he wrote that: 'a dictatorial committee composed of workers is certainly the most conceited and incompetent, and hence the most anti-revolutionary, thing that can be found . . . (It is better to have doubtful enemies in power than dubious friends)'.[6] He saw 'anarchic initiative', 'reasoned will' and 'the autonomy of each' as the conditions for the social revolution of the proletariat, the first expression of which had been the barricades of June 1848.[7] In Déjacque's view, a government resulting from an insurrection remains a reactionary fetter on the free initiative of the proletariat. Or rather, such free initiative can only arise and develop by the masses ridding themselves of the 'authoritarian prejudices' by means of which the state reproduces itself in its primary function of representation and delegation. Déjacque wrote that: 'By government I understand all delegation, all power outside the people', for which must be substituted, in a process whereby politics is transcended, the 'people in direct possession of their sovereignty', or the 'organised commune'.[8] For Déjacque, the communist anarchist utopia would fulfil the function of inciting each proletarian to explore his or her own human potentialities, in addition to correcting the ignorance of the proletarians concerning 'social science'.

However, these views on the function of the state, both in the insurrectionary period and as a mode of domination of man by man, can only be fully understood when inserted into Déjacque's global criticism of all aspects of civilisation (in the Fourierist sense of the term). For him, 'government, religion, property, family, all are linked, all coincide'.[9] The content of the social revolution was thus to be the abolition of all governments, of all religions, and of the family based on marriage, the authority of the parents and the husband, and inheritance. Also to be abolished were 'personal property, property in land, buildings, workshops, shops, property in anything that is an instrument of work, production or consumption'.[10] Déjacque's proposed abolition of property has to be understood as an attack on what is at the heart of civilisation: politics and exchange value, whose cell (in both senses) is the contract. The abolition of the state, that is to say of the political contract guaranteed by the government (legality), for which anarchy is substituted, is linked indissolubly with the abolition of commerce, that is to say of the commercial contract, which is replaced by the community of goods: 'Commerce, . . . this scourge of the 19th century, has disappeared amongst humanity. There are no longer either sellers or sold.'[11]

Déjacque's general definition of the 'anarchic community' was:

> the state of affairs where each would be free to produce and consume at will and according to their fantasy, without having to exercise or submit to any control whatsoever over anything whatever; where the balance between production and consumption would establish itself, no longer by preventive and arbitrary detention at the hands of some group or other, but by the free circulation of the faculties and needs of each.[12]

Such a definition implies a criticism of Proudhonism, that is to say of the Proudhonist version of Ricardian socialism, centred on the reward of labour power and the problem of exchange value. In his polemic with Proudhon on women's emancipation, Déjacque urged Proudhon to push on 'as far as the abolition of the contract, the abolition not only of the sword and of capital, but of property and authority in all their forms',[13] and refuted the commercial and wages logic of the demand for a 'fair reward' for 'labour' (labour power). Déjacque asked: 'Am I thus . . . right to want, as with the system of contracts, to measure out to each – according to his accidental capacity to produce – what he is entitled to?'[14] The answer given by Déjacque to this question is unambiguous: 'it is not the product of his labour that the worker has a right to, but to the satisfaction of his needs, whatever may be their nature'.[15]

The 'direct exchange' theorised by Proudhon corresponded to a supposed 'abolition' of the wages system which in fact would have turned groups of producers or individual producers into the legal agents of capital accumulation. For Déjacque, on the other hand, the communal state of affairs – the phalanstery 'without any hierarchy, without any authority' except that of the 'statistics book' – corresponded to 'natural exchange', i.e. to the 'unlimited freedom of all production and consumption; the abolition of any sign of agricultural, individual, artistic or scientific property; the destruction of any individual holding of the products of work; the demonarchisation and the demonetarisation of manual and intellectual capital as well as capital in instruments, commerce and buildings'.[16]

The abolition of exchange value depends on the answer given to the central question of 'the organisation of work' or, in other words, on the way in which those who produce are related to their activity and to the products of that activity. We have already seen that the answer Déjacque gave to the question of the distribution of products was the community of goods. But the community had first of all to be established in the sphere of productive activities themselves. Although the disappearance of all intermediaries (parasites) would allow an increase in production, and by this means would guarantee the satisfaction of needs, the essential requirement was the emancipation of the individual producer from 'enslaving subordination to the division of labour' (Marx) and, primarily, from forced labour. This is why the transformation of work into 'attractive work' was seen by Déjacque as the condition for the existence of the community: 'The organisation of attractive work by series would have replaced Malthusian competition and repulsive work.'[17] This organisation was not to be something exterior to productive activity. Déjacque's communist anthropology was based on the *liberation of needs*, including the need to act on the world and nature, and made no distinction between natural–technical necessities and human ends. Although its vocabulary was borrowed from Fourier (harmony, passions, series and so on), it aimed at the community of activities more than the organised deployment of labour power: 'The different series of workers are recruited on a voluntary basis like the men on a barricade, and are completely free to stay there as long as they want or to move on to another series or barricade.'[18] Déjacque's 'Humanisphere' was to have no hours of work nor obligatory groupings. Work could be done in isolation or otherwise.[19]

As to the division of labour, Déjacque proposed its abolition in a very original way. What he advocated was a reciprocal process of the integration of the aristocracy (or rather of the aristocratic intelligentsia) and the proletariat, each going beyond its own unilateral intellectual or manual development.

Although he recognised the futility of palliatives,[20] Déjacque was perhaps exasperated by the gulf between the results of his utopian research and the content of the class struggle in the 1850s, and tried to bridge this gulf with a theory of transition. This theory aimed to facilitate the achievement of the state of community, while taking into account the existing situation. Its three bases were, first, 'direct legislation by the people' ('the most democratic form of government, while awaiting its complete abolition'[21]); second, a range of economic measures which included 'direct exchange' (even though Déjacque admitted that this democratised property without abolishing exploitation[22]), the establishment of Owenite-type 'labour bazaars', 'circulation vouchers' (labour vouchers) and a gradual attack on property; and third, a democratisation of administrative functions (revocability of public officials, who would be paid on the basis of the average price of a day's work[23]) and the abolition of the police and the army.

It is an undeniable fact that this programme anticipated that of the Paris Commune of 1871, at least on certain points. But this is the weak side of Déjacque where he accepts the 'limits' of the 1848 revolution, against which he had exercised his critical imagination. The 'right to work' appeared along with the rest, and with it the logic of commerce. It should be noted that, on the question of the transition, Déjacque singularly lacked 'realism' since, even if the insoluble problems posed by the perspective of workers managing the process of value-capital are ignored, he proposed giving not only women but 'prisoners' and the 'insane' the right to vote, without any age limit.[24] But the transition was only a second best for Déjacque and he explicitly recognised it as such. There was no abandoning of utopian exploration in favour of the transition, but a tension between the two, the opposite to what was to be the case with Errico Malatesta, with whom he could be superficially compared.

The tenor of Déjacque's utopia, its move towards breaking with all commercial and political constraints, its desire to revive the insurrectionary energy of the proletariat, and its imaginative depth (comparable to that of William Morris) enable one to see that it made a fundamental contribution to the critical element in anarcho-communism. Déjacque provided anarcho-communism during the first cycle of its history with an iconoclastic dimension, the glimmers of which are not found again until the Kropotkin of the 1880s or until Luigi Galleani in the twentieth century.

THE REFORMULATION OF COMMUNIST ANARCHISM IN THE INTERNATIONAL WORKING MEN'S ASSOCIATION (IWMA)

The First International or International Working Men's Association was organised in 1864 and was active for several years before splitting into acrimonious factions in the aftermath of the Paris Commune of 1871. The split that occurred in the IWMA was essentially over the details of collectivism and over the ways of arriving at a 'classless society' whose necessarily anti-commercial nature was never stated (except in Marx's *Capital*), or rather never played any part in shaping the practice of the organisation. Bakunin himself, a left-wing Proudhonist for whom the abolition of exchange value would have been an aberration, purely and simply identified communism with a socialistic Jacobin tendency and, moreover, generally used the term 'authoritarian communism' as a pleonasm to describe it.

In August 1876 a pamphlet by James Guillaume entitled *Idées sur l'organisation sociale* was published in Geneva. The importance of this text lies not in its succinct presentation of the framework of a collectivist society, but in the relation set out by Guillaume between such a society and communism. Starting out from the collective ownership of the instruments of production, that is to say from the ownership by each 'corporation of workers in such and such an industry'[25] and by each agricultural grouping, and hence from the ownership by each of these groups of their own products, Guillaume ends up at 'communism', or – since he does not employ this term – at the substitution of free distribution for exchange.[26] The transition to free distribution is supposed to be organically linked to the society described by Guillaume, even though it is a society organised around the exchange of products at their value,[27] because of the guarantee represented by the collective ownership of the means of production. The essential point here is that communism is reduced to the status of a moral norm, which it would be a good thing to move towards, and is made to appear as the natural development of a collectivist (and wage) society, with its rigid division between industrial and agricultural producers, its policy of full employment and its payment of labour power.[28]

In making the precondition for communism a social relationship built on the wages system, and by seeing this as a basis for the state becoming superfluous, Guillaume laid the foundation for the regression that was to overtake anarcho-communism and of which Malatesta was to be one of the principal representatives. According to Guillaume, the preconditions for communism were a progressive appearance of an abundance of products, which would allow calculation in terms of value to be abandoned and an improvement in the 'moral sense' of the workers to occur. This in turn would enable the principle of 'free access' to be implemented. Guillaume envisaged this train of events as being brought about by the development of commercial mechanisms, with the working class acting as their recognised agent by virtue of the introduction of collective property and the guaranteed wage. What underlay all this was the implication that the act of selling is no longer anything but a simple, *technical*, transitional, rationing measure.

It was precisely in opposition to this variant of Proudhonism that anarcho-communism asserted itself in what was left of the IWMA towards the end of the 1870s. In February 1876 the Savoyard François Dumartheray (1842–1931) published in Geneva a pamphlet *Aux travailleurs manuels partisans de l'action politique*, 'corresponding to the tendencies of the section "L' Avenir", an independent group of refugees from in particular Lyons . . . For the first time anarchist communism was mentioned in a printed text.'[29] On 18 and 19 March of the same year, at a meeting organised in Lausanne by members of the IWMA and Communalists, Elisée Reclus delivered a speech in which he recognised the legitimacy of anarcho-communism. Still in 1876, a number of Italian anarchists also decided to adopt anarcho-communism, but the way they formulated this change indicated their limitations as far as the question of collectivism was concerned: 'The Italian Federation considers the collective ownership of the product of labour as the necessary complement of the collectivist programme.'[30] Also, in the spring of 1877, the *Statuten der Deutscheienden anarchischkommunistischen Partei* appeared in Berne.

The question of communism remained unsettled at the Verviers Congress of the 'anti-authoritarian' IWMA in September 1877, when the partisans of communism (Costa, Brousse) and the Spanish collectivists confronted each other, with Guillaume refusing to commit himself.[31] However, the Jura Federation, which was an anarchist grouping that had been active in the French-speaking area of Switzerland throughout the 1870s, was won over to the views of Reclus, Cafiero and Kropotkin, and integrated communism into its programme at its Congress in October 1880. At this Congress, Carlo Cafiero presented a report that was later published in *Le Révolté* under the title 'Anarchie et Communisme'. In this report, Cafiero succinctly exposed the points of rupture with collectivism: rejection of exchange value; opposition to transferring ownership of the means of production to workers' corporations; and elimination of payment for productive activities. Furthermore, Cafiero brought out the *necessary* character of communism, and hence demonstrated *the impossibility of a transitional period* of the type envisaged by Guillaume in his 1876 pamphlet. Cafiero argued that, on the one hand, the demand for the collective ownership of the means of production and 'the individual appropriation of the products of labour' would cause the accumulation of capital and the division of society into classes to reappear. On the other hand, he maintained that retaining some form of payment for individual labour power would conflict with the socialised character (indivisibility of productive activities) already imprinted on production by the capitalist mode of production. As to the need for rationing products, which might occur after the revolutionary victory, nothing would prevent such rationing from being conducted 'not according to *merits*, but according to *needs*'.[32]

Kropotkin's contribution in favour of communism at the 1880 Congress was the culmination of a slow evolution of his position from strict collectivism to communism, by way of an intermediate position where he saw collectivism as a simple transitional stage. Kropotkin's theory of anarcho-communism, which was drawn up in its essentials during the 1880s, is an elaboration of the theses presented by Cafiero in 1880 on the conditions making communism possible and on the necessity of achieving this social form, from which exchange value would disappear. Anarcho-communism is presented as a solution to crisis-ridden bourgeois society, which is torn between the underconsumption of the proletariat, underproduction and socialised labour. At the same time, anarcho-communism is seen as the realisation of tendencies towards communism and the free association of individuals which are already present in the old society. In this sense, anarcho-communism is a social form which re-establishes the principle of solidarity which exists in tribal societies.

Kropotkin's anarcho-communism has the general characteristic of being based on the satisfaction of the needs – 'necessities' and 'luxuries' – of the individual, i.e. on the 'right to well-being', as opposed to the 'right to work' and the right to the 'entire product of one's labour' which featured in the collectivists' policy of full employment and the guaranteed wage. This satisfaction of needs was to be guaranteed by a number of measures: free distribution of products was to replace commodity exchange; production was to become abundant; industrial decentralisation was to be implemented; the division of labour was to be overcome; and real economies were to be realised by the reduction of working time and the elimination of the waste caused by the capitalist mode of production. Kropotkin wrote: 'a society, having recovered the possession of all riches accumulated in its midst, can liberally assure abundance to all in return for four or five hours effective and manual work a day, as far as regards production'.[33]

Yet the question arises whether the appropriation of the instruments of production by the producers, as consumers, and by consumers, as producers, referred to a new legal form of property ownership or to the abolition of property in all its forms. Although the Anarchist Congress held in Paris in 1881 pronounced in favour of 'the abolition of all property, including collective',[34] and although Kropotkin himself contrasted 'common use' to 'ownership',[35] he still did not go beyond the collectivist perspective of the transfer of property to a new agent (i.e. for him, to society as a whole, rather than to industrial and trading commercial collectivities). Hence, he wrote: 'For association to be useful to the workers, the form of property must be changed.'[36]

The same ambiguity is found over the related question of the abolition of the division of labour. Certainly, the description which Kropotkin gave of the content of communist society in this respect is perfectly clear: integration of manual and intellectual labour; attractive and voluntary work; and fusion of agriculture, industry and art within 'industrial villages'.[37] But a revolutionary strategy which puts forward the corporatist slogan of 'The land to those who cultivate it, the factory to the workers', presupposes maintaining the division of labour and the institution of the enterprise and can be said not to go beyond the establishment of a workers' and peasants' society which would still be a form of collectivism.

The organisation of the new society, in its two aspects – communist and anarchist (in view of the necessary connection between a mode of production and its political forms) – was to be based on the 'communist commune' (rather than on the 'free commune' of the Communalists),[38] federalism (decentralisation and economic self-sufficiency of regions or producing areas) and neighbourhood assemblies.[39] Kropotkin distinguished three possible methods of organisation: on a territorial basis (federation of independent communes); on the basis of social function (federation of trades); and that to which he gave all his attention, and which he hoped would expand, on the basis of personal affinity. In fact, the 'free and spontaneous grouping of men functioning in harmony'[40] seemed to him to be the essential characteristic of the particular social relationship of anarcho-communism.

But the important point lies more in the forms and content of the revolutionary process, of which all this was to be the end result. The revolution was seen as an international process, starting with a long period of insurrection, whose model Kropotkin found in the repeated peasant insurrections that had preceded the French Revolution. Such a revolutionary process would end in a phase of general expropriation, which would mark the beginning of 'the reconstruction of society':

> Expropriation, such then is the problem which history has put before the men of the twentieth century: the return to Communism in all that ministers to the well-being of man. . . by taking immediate and effective posession of all that is necessary to ensure the well-being of all.[41]

Immediate expropriation defined the whole logic of the revolutionary process for Kropotkin. Basically, it is here that the essence of his work lies. The real answer to the objections that can be made against him (regarding his optimistic assumptions about human nature, the abundance of products and so on) lies in the alternatives which he posed: *either* the immediate communisation of social relations *or* the wages system in one form or another.[42] If proof of the stark nature of these alternatives was ever required, history has provided such proof in abundance.

For Kropotkin, the critique of the wages sytem was indissolubly linked with a critique of collectivism (Proudhonist or Guesdist). He wrote: 'The most prominent characteristic of our present capitalism is *the wage system.*'[43] Kropotkin saw the wages system as presupposing the separation of the producers from the means of production and as being based on the principle 'to each according to his deeds':

> It was by proclaiming this principle that wagedom began, to end in the glaring inequalities and all the abominations of present society; because, from the moment work done began to be appraised in currency, or in any other form of wage . . . the whole history of a State-aided Capitalist Society was as good as written.[44]

The collectivists favoured the 'right to work', which is 'industrial penal servitude'. In Kropotkin's view, their pro-worker policy sought to 'harness to the same cart the wages system and collective ownership',[45] in particular through their theory of labour vouchers. Kropotkin opposed labour vouchers on the grounds that they seek to measure the exact value of labour in an economy which, being socialised, tends to eliminate all distinctions as far as the contribution of each worker considered in isolation is concerned. Furthermore, the existence of labour vouchers would continue to make society 'a commercial company based on *debit* and *credit*'.[46] Hence he denounced labour vouchers in the following terms: 'The idea . . . is old. It dates from Robert Owen. Proudhon advocated it in 1848. Today, it has become "scientific socialism".'[47]

Kropotkin made equally stringent criticisms of the collectivists' attitudes towards the division of labour and the state. With regard to the division of labour, he wrote: 'Talk to them [the collectivist socialists] about the organization of work during the Revolution, and they answer that the division of labour must be maintained.'[48] As for the state, it was significant that as soon as Kropotkin had come out in favour of 'direct, immediate communist anarchism at the moment of the social revolution',[49] he criticised the Paris Commune as an example of a revolution where, in the absence of the communist perspective, the proletariat had become bogged down in problems of power and representation.[50] Kropotkin believed that the Paris Commune illustrated well how the 'revolutionary state' acts as a *substitute for communism* and provides a new form of domination linked to the wages system. In contrast to this, 'it is by revolutionary socialist acts, by abolishing individual property, that the Communes of the coming revolution will affirm and establish their independence'.[51] Further, communism would transform the nature of the Commune itself:

> For us, 'Commune' is no longer a territorial agglomeration; it is rather a generic noun, synonym of a grouping of equals which knows neither frontiers nor walls. The social commune will soon cease to be a clearly-defined whole.[52]

For Kropotkin, what characterises the revolutionary process is, in the first place, general expropriation, the taking possession of all 'riches' (means of production, products, houses and so on), with the aim of immediately improving the material situation of the whole population. He wrote: 'with this watchword of *Bread for All* the Revolution will triumph'.[53] Since Kropotkin foresaw that a revolution would in the beginning make millions of proletarians unemployed, the solution would be to take over the whole of production so as to ensure the satisfaction of needs (and not the reproduction of the wages sytem). More precisely, the social nature of the revolution had to show itself in its capacity to ensure the satisfaction of food and clothing needs. First of all, the population 'should take immediate possession of all the food of the insurgent communes',[54] draw up an inventory, and organise a provisions service by streets and districts which would distribute food free, on the principle: 'no stint or limit to what the community possesses in abundance, but equal sharing and dividing of those things which are scarce or apt to run short'.[55] As for housing:

> If the people of the Revolution expropriate the houses and proclaim free lodgings – the communalizing of houses and the right of each family to a decent dwelling – then the Revolution will have assumed a communistic character from the first. . . the expropriation of dwellings contains in germ the whole social revolution.[56]

A second characteristic of Kropotkin's vision of the revolutionary process was to integrate the countryside into the process of communisation, by making an agreement 'with the factory workers, the necessary raw materials given them, and the means of subsistence assured to them, while they worked to supply the needs of the agricultural population'.[57] Kropotkin regarded the integration of town and country as of fundamental importance, since it bore on the necessity to ensure the subsistence of the population and would be accompanied by the beginning of the abolition of the division of labour, starting from the industrial centres. He thought that 'The large towns, as well as the villages, must undertake to till the soil',[58] in a process of improvement and extension of cultivated areas. In Kropotkin's view, the agrarian question was thus decisive right from the beginning of the revolution. Kropotkin's exposition of the expropriation of the land for the benefit of society (the land to belong to everyone) was not, however, free from the ambiguity we mentioned above. To make land – as with all else – a property question[59] amounts to placing productive activity above the satisfaction of needs, to inserting a social actor between the population and the satisfaction of their needs. Property can only be private.

This inability to break definitively with collectivism in all its forms also exhibited itself over the question of the workers' movement, which divided anarcho-communism into a number of tendencies. To say that the industrial and agricultural proletariat is the natural bearer of the revolution and communisation does not tell us under what form it is or should be so. In the theory of the revolution which we have just summarised, it is the risen people who are the real agent and not the working class organised in the enterprises (the cells of the capitalist mode of production) and seeking to assert itself as labour power, as a more 'rational' industrial body and/or social brain (manager) than the employers. Between 1880 and 1890, the anarcho-communists, with their perspective of an imminent revolution, were opposed to the official workers' movement which was then in the process of formation (general Social Democratisation). They were opposed not only to political (statist) struggles but also to strikes which put forward wage or other claims, or which were organised by trade unions. While they were not opposed to strikes as such, they were opposed to trade unions and the struggle for the eight-hour day. This anti-reformist tendency was accompanied by an anti-organisation tendency, and its partisans declared themselves in favour of agitation amongst the unemployed for the expropriation of foodstuffs and other articles, for the expropriatory strike and, in some cases, for 'individual recuperation' or acts of terrorism.

From the 1890s, however, the anarcho-communists, and Kropotkin in particular, were to begin to integrate themselves directly into the logic of the workers' movement (reproduction of waged labour power). In 1890 Kropotkin 'was one of the first to declare the urgency of "entering the trade unions"',[60] as a means of trying to overcome the dilemma in which, according to him, anarcho-communism risked trapping itself. Kropotkin saw this dilemma in terms of *either* joining with the reformist workers' movement *or* sterile and sectarian withdrawal. 'Workmen's organisations are the real force capable of accomplishing the social revolution', he was to declare later.[61]

Coinciding with the birth of anarcho-syndicalism and revolutionary unionism, three tendencies emerged within anarcho-communism. First, there was the tendency represented by Kropotkin himself and *Les Temps Nouveaux* (Jean Grave). Second, there were a number of groups which were influenced by Kropotkin but which were less reserved than him towards the trade unions (for example, *Khleb i Volia* in Russia). Finally, there were the anti-syndicalist anarcho-communists, who in France were grouped around Sebastien Faure's *Le Libertaire*.[62] From 1905 onwards, the Russian counterparts of these anti-syndicalist anarcho-communists became partisans of economic terrorism and illegal 'expropriations'.[63]

Certainly, it would be an 'illusion to seek to discover or to create a syndicalist Kropotkin',[64] at least in the strict sense of the term, if only because he rejected the theory of the trade union as the embryo of future society – which did not prevent him from writing a preface in 1911 for the book written by the anarcho-syndicalists Emile Pataud and Emile Pouget, *Syndicalism and the Co-operative Commonwealth (How We Shall Bring About the Revolution)*.[65] But he saw the trade-union movement as a natural milieu for agitation, which it would be possible to *use* in the attempt to find a solution to the reformism/sectarianism dilemma. As an alternative to the strategy of the Russian 'illegalist' anarcho-communists, Kropotkin envisaged the formation of independent anarchist trade unions whose aim would be to counteract the influence of the Social Democrats. He defined his strategy in one sentence in the 1904 introduction to the Italian edition of *Paroles d'un révolté*: 'Expropriation as the aim, and the general strike as the means to paralyse the bourgeois world in all countries at the same time.'[66]

At the end of his life Kropotkin seems to have abandoned his previous reservations and to have gone so far as to see in syndicalism the only 'groundwork for the reconstruction of Russia's economy'.[67] In May 1920, he declared that: 'the syndicalist movement . . . will emerge as the great force in the course of the next fifty years, leading to the creation of the communist stateless society'.[68] He was equally optimistic about the prospects facing the cooperative movement. Remarks such as these opened the way for the theoretical regression which was to make anarcho-communism a simple variant of anarcho-syndicalism, based on the collective management of enterprises. Reduced to the level of caricature, 'anarcho-communism' even became an empty phrase like the Spanish 'libertarian communism' of the 1930s, to say nothing of the contemporary use to which this latter term is put.

THE END OF ANARCHO-COMMUNISM?

Kropotkin's last contribution, not to anarcho-communism but to its transformation into an ideology, was the introduction of the mystifying concept of Russian 'state communism'. Faced with the events of the Russian Revolution and the establishment of a capitalist state freed from the fetters of Tsarism, Kropotkin should logically have seen the new state as a form of collectivism. He should have recognised that its character was determined by the wages system, as with other varieties of collectivism which he had previously exposed. In fact, he limited himself to criticising the Bolsheviks' methods, without drawing attention to the fact that the object towards which those methods were directed had nothing to do with communism. A good example of this is the question which he directed at Lenin in the autumn of 1920:

> Are you so blinded, so much a prisoner of your authoritarian ideas, that you do not realise that, being at the head of European Communism, you have no right to soil the ideas which you defend by shameful methods . . . ?[69]

After Kropotkin's death, the *theory* of anarcho-communism survived, but was consigned to isolation by the unfolding counter-revolution from the 1920s onwards. Unlike the Italian Left and the German-Dutch council communists (the latter above all, with their criticism of the whole workers' movement and their analysis of the general tendency for a unification of labour, capital and the state), the partisans of anarcho-communism did not really try to discover the causes of this counter-revolution; nor did they perceive its extent. As a result, their contributions amounted to little more than a formal defence of principles, without any critical depth. Moreover, these contributions ceased very rapidly. Sebastien Faure's *Mon Communisme* appeared in 1921, Luigi Galleani's *The End of Anarchism?* in 1925 and Alexander Berkman's *What Is Communist Anarchism?* (better known in its abridged form as the *ABC of Anarchism*) in 1929.[70]

From this date on, if we exclude the minority current in the General Confederation of Labour, Revolutionary Syndicalist (CGTSR), whose positions were made clear by Gaston Britel,[71] the critical force that anarcho-communism had represented left the anarchist movement to reappear with the dissident Bordigist Raoul Brémond (see his *La Communauté*, which was first published in 1938)[72] and certain communist currents that arose in the 1970s. Representative of these latter was the group which published in Paris in 1975 the pamphlet

Un Monde sans argent: le communisme, which is discussed in Chapter 6.

As a *practical* movement, anarcho-communism came to an end in Mexico and Russia. In Mexico before the First World War, the Partido Liberal Mexicano (PLM) of the brothers Enrique and Ricardo Florès Magon, supported by a movement of peasants and Indians which aimed to expropriate the land, tried to achieve anarcho-communism.[73] The PLM's objective was to revive the community traditions of the *ejidos* – common lands – and ultimately to extend the effects of this essentially agrarian rebellion to the industrial areas. The PLM came to control the greater part of Lower California and was joined by a number of IWW 'Wobblies' and Italian anarchists. But it was unable to implement its project of agricultural cooperatives organised on anarcho-communist principles and was eventually defeated militarily.

The 1917 revolution in Russia gave impetus to a process that had begun before, whereby anarcho-communism was absorbed or replaced by anarcho-syndicalism. In addition to this, in certain cases anarcho-communists allowed themselves to be integrated into the Bolshevik state. It is true that a few groups refused all support, even 'critical', for the Bolsheviks and combated them with terrorism, but they experienced increasing isolation. For the last time in the twentieth century a social movement of some size – in particular in Petrograd where the Federation of Anarchists (Communists) had considerable influence before the summer of 1917, the date when the exiled syndicalists returned – consciously proposed to remove 'government and property, prisons and barracks, money and profit' and usher in 'a stateless society with a "natural economy"'.[74] But their programme of systematic expropriations (as opposed to workers' control), 'embracing houses and food, factories and farms, mines and railroads', was limited in reality to several anarcho-communist groups after the February Revolution expropriating 'a number of private residences in Petrograd, Moscow, and other cities'.[75]

As for the Makhnovist insurrectionary movement, although it was in favour of communism in the long run,[76] and although it declared that 'all forms of the wages system must be irredeemably abolished',[77] it nevertheless drew up a transitional programme which preserved the essential features of the commodity economy within a framework of cooperatives. Wages, comparison of products in terms of value, taxes, a 'decentralised system of genuine people's banks' and direct trade between workers were all in evidence in this transitional programme.[78]

As a conclusion, we will recall Kropotkin's warning: 'The Revolution must be communist or it will be drowned in blood.'[79]

Notes

1. See J. Rancière and A. Faure, *La Parole ouvrière, 1830–1851* (Paris: Union générale, 1976) pp. 268–78.
2. Quoted in Max Nettlau, *Histoire de l'anarchie, Les dossiers de l'histoire* (Paris: Editions de l'Université et de l'Enseignement moderne, 1983) p. 76.
3. Joseph Déjacque, *La Question révolutionnaire* (1854), in Joseph Déjacque, *A bas les chefs!* (Paris: Champ Libre, 1970) p. 67. Elsewhere Déjacque speaks of 'the illogicality of being communist and authoritarian' (Déjacque, 1970, p. 245).
4. Déjacque, 1970, p.215.
5. Ibid, p. 215.
6. Ibid, p. 217.
7. Ibid, p. 219.
8. Ibid, pp. 45–7.
9. Ibid, p. 70.
10. Quoted in V. Pelosse, 'J. Déjacque et la création du néologisme "libertaire" (1857)', *Etudes de Marxologie*, VI (December 1972) p. 2366.
11. Joseph Déjacque, *L'Humanisphère, utopie anarchique* (1858), in Déjacque, 1970, p. 184.
12. Joseph Déjacque, *De l'être humain mâle et femelle. Lettre à P. J. Proudhon* (1857), quoted in Pelosse, 1972, p. 2358.
13. Ibid, p. 2358. Déjacque's views on this question remain ambivalent, however, since he speaks elsewhere of 'collective property' in respect of the community (Déjacque, 1970, p. 66).
14. Pelosse, 1972, pp. 2358–9.
15. Ibid, p. 2365. See also Déjacque, 1970, p. 177.
16. *Le Libertaire*, 6 (1858), quoted in Pelosse, 1972, p. 2365. See also Déjacque, 1970, p. 157.
17. Déjacque, *La Question révolutionnaire*, in Déjacque, 1970, p. 67.
18. Déjacque, *L'Humanisphère*, in Déjacque, 1970, p. 189.
19. Ibid, p. 151.
20. Déjacque, 1970, p. 267.
21. Déjacque, *La Question révolutionnaire*, in Déjacque, 1970, p. 48.

22. Pelosse, 1972. p. 2366.
23. Déjacque, *La Question révolutionnaire*, in Déjacque, 1970, p. 52.
24. Ibid, pp. 54–5.
25. James Guillaume, *Idées sur l'organisation sociale* (Paris: *Volonté Anarchiste*, no. 8 – Edition du groupe Fresnes-Antony de la Fédération anarchiste, 1979) p. 15.
26. Ibid, p. 22.
27. Ibid, pp. 20–1.
28. Ibid, p. 13.
29. Nettlau, 1983, p. 140.
30. Ibid, p. 141.
31. Ibid, p. 142.
32. C. Cafiero, 'Anarchie et Communisme'. Republished under the title *Communisme et Anarchisme* (Paris: Groupe Eugène Varlin de la Fédération anarchiste, 1982) p. 7 (emphases in the original).
33. Peter Kropotkin, *Anarchism: Its Philosophy and Ideal*, in Roger N. Baldwin, *Kropotkin's Revolutionary Pamphlets* (New York: Dover, 1970) p. 129.
34. *Le Révolté* (June 1881), quoted in J. Maîtron, *Histoire du mouvement anarchiste en France*, vol. I (Paris: Maspero, 1978) p. 112.
35. Martin A. Miller, *Kropotkin* (Chicago: University Press, 1976) p. 145.
36. Pierre Kropotkine, *Fatalité de la révolution* (Toulouse: Editions CNT, 1975) p. 15.
37. See Peter Kropotkin, *Fields, Factories and Workshops* (New York: Greenwood, 1968), and Peter Kropotkin, *The Conquest of Bread* (New York: University Press, 1972) pp. 137ff.
38. Pierre Alekseievitch Kropotkine, *Paroles d'un révolté* (Paris: Flammarion, 1978) pp. 93, 97.
39. Nettlau, 1983, p. 250.
40. Elisée Reclus, *L'Homme et la terre*, vol. II (Paris: Maspero, 1982) pp. 140–1.
41. Kropotkin, 1972, pp. 55 and 59.
42. Ibid, p. 195.
43. Ibid, p. 87 (emphasis in the original).
44. Ibid, pp. 183–4.
45. Kropotkine, 1978, p. 110.
46. Kropotkin, 1972, p. 187 (emphases in the original).
47. Pierre Kropotkine, *L'Anarchie, sa philosophie, son idéal* (Paris: Publico, 1981) p. 22.
48. Kropotkin, 1972, p. 198.
49. Nettlau, 1983, p. 145.
50. Pierre Kropotkine, 'La Commune de Paris', in *Le Révolté* (March 1880), reproduced in Kropotkine, 1978, pp. 103ff.
51. Kropotkine, 1978, p. 113.
52. Ibid, p. 101.
53. Kropotkin, 1972, p. 84.
54. Ibid, p. 87.
55. Ibid, p. 92. (We have changed the word 'commodities' in the English translation to 'things' since Kropotkin did not use the term 'commodities' in the original French.)

56. Ibid, pp. 110–11.
57. Ibid, p. 87.
58. Ibid, p. 103.
59. See Kropotkine, 1978, p. 119.
60. Maîtron, 1978, p. 266.
61. *Les Temps Nouveaux* (25 May 1907), quoted in G. Woodcock and I. Avakumovič, *The Anarchist Prince* (London: Boardman, 1950) p. 294.
62. From its foundation in 1895 up till 1899, *Le Libertaire* adopted a hostile attitude to trade unions. After 1899 it moved towards syndicalism. In his *Mon Communisme* Faure attributed an important role to trade unions, both in the insurrectionary phase and in the organisation of non-commercial social relations. The division of labour was also to be maintained within the framework of a non-monetary economy. (Sebastien Faure, *Mon Communisme* (Paris: Editions de 'La Fraternelle', 1921).)
63. For example, the brothers Abram and Iouda Solomonovich Grossman held that mass expropriation ought to replace strikes and saw in the unions a tendency towards the formation of a new 'ruling aristocracy'. For anti-syndicalists like the Grossmans, anarcho-communist society was envisaged as something quite different from 'a society of massive industrial complexes managed by trade unions'. Indeed, they argued that the revolution should aim to destroy the unions, along with all other capitalist and statist institutions. (See Paul Avrich, *The Russian Anarchists* (Princeton: University Press, 1967) pp. 84–9.)
64. Nettlau, 1983, p. 232.
65. Emile Pataud and Emile Pouget, *Syndicalism and the Co-operative Commonwealth. How We Shall Bring About the Revolution* (Oxford: New International, 1913).
66. Kropotkine, 1978, p. 263.
67. Avrich, 1967, p. 226.
68. Ibid, p. 227.
69. Quoted in Woodcock and Avakumovič, 1950, p. 427.
70. Luigi Galleani, *The End of Anarchism?*(Sanday: Cienfuegos, 1982); Alexander Berkman, *What Is Communist Anarchism?* (New York: Vanguard, 1929). As for Malatesta, he never went beyond James Guillaume's *Idées sur l'organisation sociale*, since he made the conditions for the existence of communism (abundance and a spirit of solidarity) a justification for collectivism. Hence collectivism ceased to appear as a form of the wages system and could be integrated into the *ideology* of anarchism as 'free experimentation'. See, for example, Errico Malatesta, *Articles politiques* (Paris: Union générale d'éditions 10/18, 1979) pp. 210, 381; *Ecrits choisis*, vol. II (Annecy: Groupe ler Mai, 1981) pp. 58–9, 63.
71. Gaston Britel, *La Foire aux ânes ou de l'Abolition du salariat* (no place: Editions de la Moisson Nouvelle, 1951). This is a collection of texts, the earliest of which dates from the late 1930s.
72. Raoul Brémond, *La Communauté* (Paris: Editions de l'Oubli, 1975).
73. See its anti-commercial programme, Manifesto of 23 September 1911, in R. F. Magon, *Land and Liberty: Anarchist Influences in the Mexican Revolution* (Sanday: Cienfuegos, 1977) pp. 99–100.

74. Avrich, 1967, p. 126.
75. Ibid, pp. 126 and 130.
76. See the draft Declaration of the Insurrectionary Army of the Ukraine (Makhnovist), adopted by the revolutionary military Soviet at its meeting of 20 October 1919, in Alexandre Skirda, *Nestor Makhno, le Cosaque de l'Anarchie* (Paris: Skirda, 1982) p. 442.
77. Ibid, p. 447.
78. Ibid, pp. 200–1, 210, 448–9.
79. Pierre Kropotkine, *Le Salariat* (1911), reissued by Le 'Combat Syndicaliste' (Paris: 1973) p. 11.

4 Impossibilism

Stephen Coleman

Like other terms of political abuse which have been absorbed into our political vocabulary, the term 'impossibilism' tells us as much or more about the labellers as it does about the idea being described. After the French legislative election of October 1881, in which the Marxist Fédération du Parti des Travailleurs Socialistes de France won only 60 000 of the 7 million votes cast, a group based around Paul Brousse and Benoît Malon began to advocate a more pragmatic, reformist policy for the Fédération. 'We prefer to abandon the "all-at-once" tactics practised until now', proclaimed those who referred to themselves as Possibilists. 'We desire to divide our ideal ends into several gradual stages, to make many of our demands immediate ones and hence *possible* of realisation.'[1] The Possibilists regarded socialism as a progressive social process rather than an 'all-at-once' end. Those who regarded capitalism and socialism as mutually exclusive systems and refused to budge from the revolutionary position of what has become known as 'the maximum programme' were labelled as impossibilists.[2]

It did not take very long for the term to find its way into British use. For example, in 1896 Ramsay MacDonald, in urging 'socialists more frequently to put themselves in the position of the man in the street', warned that:

> We can talk socialism seriously to him and we will likely disgust him; we may gas sentimentalities to him and we may capture a member who will only be one more impossibilist in our movement.[3]

While MacDonald and the Independent Labour Party (ILP) pursued the propaganda of condescension, assured in their own minds that the presentation to workers of the revolutionary alternative to capitalism would cause disgust, the majority of the members of the nominally Marxist Social Democratic Federation (SDF), led by the dogmatic capitalist, H. M. Hyndman, moved increasingly towards the possibilist policies of parliamentary reformism and opportunist party-building within the trade unions. At the turn of the century a small group within the SDF – some based in Scotland, some in London, but numbering no more than 400 out of the membership of 9 000 – began to oppose the Federation's drift towards possibilism. The story of the impossibilist revolt need not be repeated here; it is sufficient to point out that the leadership of the SDF pursued a minor purge against those who insisted that the Federation should stand for clear-cut non-market socialism and nothing less.[4] T. A. Jackson refers to the expulsion of Jack Fitzgerald as 'a trumped up charge',[5] and the obituary of Fitzgerald, published in the *Socialist Standard* in May 1929, commented upon the fact that he:

> was jeered at by the official group, who tried to silence him by the charge of 'impossibilism'. He, and the group that was with him, were confronted by a solid wall of opposition, which was the more difficult to get over because the officials held the strings, and meetings were closed to the unauthorised.

The most typically impossibilist and historically enduring product of the split in the SDF emerged in 1904 when the majority of the London impossibilists, having exhausted the possibilities of turning the SDF away from its reformist course, formed a new party: the Socialist Party of Great Britain (SPGB). Although labelled by opponents as impossibilists (a term which we now use solely for historical reference and not because we have any sympathy with the assumptions upon which it is based), as in the SDF paper *Justice*, the workers who formed the SPGB rejected the label and its implicit accusation:

> At the outset let us insist that we do not believe in impossible political tactics. None the less, our political action must be such as to awaken the workers of this country to full class-consciousness, and to the desire to abolish wage slavery. We therefore feel the necessity of avoiding any action that will endanger or obliterate our socialist identity, or allow us to be swallowed up by a Labour Movement which has yet to learn the real meaning of Class Struggle.[6]

> We are not . . . 'Impossibilists', if *Justice*'s definition be correct, but we doubt its correctness, for we have usually seen what is described as 'Impossibilism' associated with Socialist science, working-class sincerity and correct tactics.[7]

In fact, the SPGB contended that the real impossibilists were the self-proclaimed realists who sought to humanise capitalism by means of legislative reform.[8]

Before considering the non-market socialist outlook of the SPGB – and of the parties and individuals in other parts of the world adhering to its principles – there are two other groups which deserve to be examined briefly as examples of impossibilism in Britain.

WILLIAM MORRIS AND THE SOCIALIST LEAGUE

The Socialist League split from the SDF in December 1884 in circumstances which closely resembled the impossibilist revolt two decades later.[9] Hyndman asserted that the 'antagonism' between the SDF and the League was 'similar to that which existed in France between the Marxists and the Possibilists', and although the arrogant Hyndman cast the SDF in the role of the Marxists, the analogy is, in fact, appropriate insofar as the SDF was comparable to the Possibilists and the League represented impossibilism.[10] The League rejected the idea of having a reform programme, like the 'Stepping Stones' of the SDF. William Morris, who fed the best revolutionary ideas into the League, declared that 'The palliatives over which many worthy people are busying themselves now are useless.'[11] Morris's conception of socialism, which he advocated both in the League and in the years after he left it, was characterised by an awareness – uncommon amongst those claiming to be socialists, both then and now – of the nature of the social transformation which socialism would entail. Socialism would 'put an end for ever to the wage-system';[12] it would allow everyone to have 'free access to the means of production of wealth';[13] it would 'not know the meaning of the words rich and poor, or the rights of property, or law or legality, or nationality';[14] and, if *News From Nowhere* is a guide to Morris's conception of socialism, it will be a moneyless society in which the 'extinct commercial morality' of buying and selling relationships will be utterly incomprehensible to anyone but historians.[15] These features of non-market socialism are presented by Morris with a particular clarity of vision and experiential relevance, in a way that makes it hard to understand without at the same time desiring the nature of the social revolution which he is proposing. A particular quality of Morris's conception of socialism, comparable in certain respects with the situationists of the following century, was his eagerness to relate to the down-to-earth concerns of workers. Above all, Morris saw what work could be like in a society which no longer sacrificed creative labour to commercial profit:

> *all* work is now pleasurable; either because of the hope of gain in honour and wealth with which the work is done, which causes pleasurable excitement, even when the actual work is not pleasant; or else because it has grown into a pleasurable *habit*, as in the case with what you may call mechanical work; and lastly (and most of our work is of this kind) because there is conscious sensuous pleasure in the work itself; it is done, that is, by artists.[16]

That Morris was dismissed as a utopian dreamer by many self-styled socialists in his own day and since, tells us more about their conservatism than his vision. As Karl Mannheim commented, with a relevance to the concept of impossibilism of which he was not aware: 'The representatives of a given order will label as utopian all conceptions of existence which *from their point of view* can in principle never be realized.'[17]

Unlike the SPGB, which was to accept Morris's general picture of socialism as an immediately realisable objective, Morris himself and the Socialist League asserted that such a system could only be established after a period of transition. Morris's transition period was conceived as being a society in which property would still exist and in 'which currency will still be used as a means of exchange'.[18] Such a transition was not envisaged as being a long-lasting phase,[19] but the idea of a society of property and exchange relationships being defined as socialist – albeit qualified by the adjective 'incomplete' – must be regarded as an abuse of the term. We are not here disputing the fact that such a transition might have been necessary in the last century (Marx certainly considered that it was[20]), but that is no excuse for creating the conceptual confusion of regarding the pre-socialist transition period as the first stage of socialism.

DANIEL DELEON AND THE SOCIALIST LABOUR PARTY

The same criticism must be levelled against the Socialist Labour Party (SLP), which broke away from the SDF a year before the SPGB. This party modelled its ideas on the industrial unionist policy of Daniel DeLeon and the American SLP. Like the Socialist League and the SPGB, the mainly Scottish impossibilists who formed the SLP advanced a conception of non-market socialism which can be seen to fall within the tradition of thought being considered in this book. But, while stating that 'There will be no money under Socialism', the SLP goes on to state that:

> With the establishment of a system of production-for-use, labor-time vouchers, which the workers may exchange for goods and services, will take the place of money.
>
> Accordingly, under Socialism the worker will receive a labor-time voucher from his union showing that he has worked a certain number of hours. This time voucher will enable him to withdraw from the social store as much as he contributed to it, after the necessary deductions are made for replacement of wornout equipment, expansion of production, schools, parks, public health etc.[21]

An economy based on labour-vouchers would, in effect, be a non-socialist society: first, because the law of value would still exist, measuring the worth of labour input and allowing certain amounts of goods and services to be used on the basis of equivalent value (no mention is made of those who do not work); second, because the limitation of access to the common store by means of vouchers could easily lead to the circulation of vouchers, which would be in effect monetary circulation; and finally, because the absence of free access on the basis of self-defined needs and self-restraint (where materially necessary) imposes a form of economic alienation which is incompatible with the freedom of a non-exchange society sought by socialists. As early as 1918 the SLP (in Scotland) published Marx's *Critique of the Gotha Programme* under the title of *The Socialist Programme*. In that work Marx makes the case for the use of labour vouchers in the very early days of socialism, but points out that 'these defects' will be transcended when 'the productive forces have also increased with the all-round development of the individual, and all the springs of co-operative wealth flow more abundantly'.[22] The case for the immediate abolition of the law of value and its monetary expression is argued by the SPGB, which rejects the relevance of Marx's ideas about labour vouchers,[23] while the SLP (no longer active in Britain, but still existing in the USA) persists in advocating a form of 'socialism' without free access. It must be emphasised that the SLP's abuse of the concept of socialism is more serious than that of the Socialist League, for in the latter case it was at least proposed that labour vouchers would exist only in the brief transition period, while the SLP sees a need for such a rationing system within the period that Morris might have called 'complete socialism'.

Having criticised the SLP on one crucial point, it can still be said that it and other DeLeonists have made an outstanding contribution during the course of the century to propaganda in favour of the abolition of class monopoly and wage labour. Between 1903 and 1917, in addition to its very limited success in the creation of socialist trade unions, the SLP in Britain did valuable work in providing basic Marxist education for workers. After the Bolshevik *coup d'état* of 1917 one section of the SLP turned enthusiastically to Bolshevism (even though they were criticised by Lenin for taking Bolshevik propaganda at its face value[24]), while those who rejected the Bolshevik tactics maintained a dwindling party in Britain until quite recently. Today in the USA the DeLeonist movement has split in different directions, with journals like *The Socialist Republic* and *The Industrial Unionist*, as well as *The People*, published by the SLP, providing valuable analyses of the class struggle.

THE SOCIALIST PARTY OF GREAT BRITAIN

In June 1904 the Socialist Party of Great Britain adopted an Object and Declaration of Principles which it has not since changed. In September of that year the first issue of the *Socialist Standard* was published and the Object and Declaration of Principles have appeared in every monthly issue since then – not a single month's publication having ever been missed, despite the difficult circumstances of two world wars and frequent financial crises. Consistency has been the hallmark of the SPGB – a persistence of outlook which has infuriated, intrigued and won respect from those aware of it. The ideas of the Party have travelled: parties in Australia, New Zealand, Canada, the USA and Ireland, groups in Austria, Sweden and France, and active supporters as far apart as Jamaica, India and Hong Kong hold tight not only to the principles of the Party (which refers to itself internationally as the World Socialist Movement), but also to a certain political style which steers an unsteady course between uncompromising clarity and doctrinaire intolerance.

The Object shared by the SPGB and the other parties and groups of the World Socialist Movement does not tell us in much detail what they stand for:

> The establishment of a system of society based upon the common ownership and democratic control of the means and instruments for producing and distributing wealth by and in the interest of the whole community.

Nor do the eight principles offer great help in outlining the non-market socialist aim: in Clause 3 the points made in the Object are repeated in different words; Clause 4 makes it clear that socialist emancipation will be 'without distinction of race or sex' (an advanced proposition for 1904); and Clause 8 refers to 'comfort', 'equality' and 'freedom' as being benefits to be gained in socialism. The SPGB has traditionally shared Marx's caution about devising utopian blueprints for socialism. None the less, much more has been said and written by SPGB-style impossibilists about socialism than is to be found in the Object and Principles. In his *20th Century World Socialist or Communist Manifesto*, published in 1951, M. J. Panicker explains that:

> Socialism is a universal system of society where there will be no buying and selling. Consequently all institutions which are now functioning only for the running of this buying and selling will disappear. Money, banks, insurance

> companies and several other institutions will disappear. All the resources of the world, the means and instruments of wealth production and social services necessary to the sustenance of mankind will be held in common by the whole people of the community as you and I breathe air or drink water. All the people will happily work and they will have free access to their needs. Each and everyone will determine his own needs.[25]

Panicker has spent years advocating these ideas in India. It is accepted by all SPGB-impossibilists that socialism will entail the immediate ending of the capital / wage-labour relationship:

> there can be no wages system. Wages, of course, mean that somebody is working for somebody else – they imply rich and poor, two classes. To talk of wages under socialism is ridiculous.[26]

Similarly, it is seen as being ridiculous to speak of the existence of money in a society of common ownership. In 1943 two chemists by the name of Phillips and Renson (writing under the name of Philoren) wrote an excellent book introducing the idea of socialism (without using the term socialism) entitled *Money Must Go*; in it they argued that:

> What I do propose is, that the whole system of money and exchange, buying and selling, profit-making and wage-earning should be entirely abolished and that instead, the community as a whole should organise and administer the production of goods for use only, and the free distribution of these goods to all the members of the community according to each person's needs.[27]

What about the state? Long before widespread nationalisation took place in Britain, the SPGB had pointed out 'how little difference there is from the workers' point of view between State capitalism and private capitalism, whether under a Conservative or a Labour government'.[28] According to the SPGB, socialism will be a stateless society:

> The State, which is an organisation composed of soldiers, policemen, judges, and gaolers charged with enforcing the laws, is only needed in class society, for in such societies there is no community of interest, only class conflict. The

> purpose of government is to maintain law and order in the interests of the dominant class. It is in fact an instrument of class oppression. In Socialism there will be no classes and no built-in class conflicts . . . The phrase 'socialist government' is a contradiction in terms. Where there is Socialism there is no government and where there is government there is no Socialism.[29]

A distinction between government and democratic administration is made. The SPGB has tended to refrain from extensive speculation about the precise organisation of the stateless society, pointing out that such decisions must be made by those establishing socialism, in accordance, no doubt, with ideas and plans formulated in the course of the revolutionary process. Many different kinds of bodies *might* be used by the inhabitants of socialist society:

> there is intrinsically nothing wrong with institutions where delegates assemble to parley (Parliaments, congresses, diets or even so-called soviets). What is wrong with them today is that such parliaments are controlled by the capitalist class. Remove class society and the assemblies will function in the interest of the whole people.[30]

Advocates of soviets or council communism will note that their insistence upon how socialism would have to be organised is not ruled out by the SPGB. The point emphasised is that those establishing socialism will be free to determine the nature of its administration. Of course, such a decision will not be based upon utopian fancy, but will have to accord with the historical circumstances existing at the time of the revolution:

> The basis of industrial organisation and administration will start from the arrangements existing under Capitalism at the time of the transformation, and this will present no difficulties because the Socialist movement will already be thoroughly international, both in outlook and practical organisation. As far as the machinery of organisation and administration is concerned, it will be local, regional, national and international, evolving out of existing forms.[31]

The quotations given demonstrate clearly that the essential features of non-market socialism are advocated unequivocally by the SPGB and those sharing its principles. One does not have to search long to find within such literature clear and simple statements of what socialism means. Indeed, one strength of impossibilist literature is its tendency to get to the point. Perhaps at the cost of being repetitive – and after eighty years that is forgivable – the SPGB remembers (usually, at least) to address itself to the uninitiated who do not want to read about one hundred new positions before they have been told the facts of life. Poets write stirring poetry and philosophers polemicise well, but it takes a straight talker to deliver a plain and urgent message; even its enemies have never accused the SPGB of being other than straight talkers.

CONSCIOUSNESS AND DEMOCRACY

Two political terms which are important in explaining the SPGB position are Consciousness and Democracy. This is because of the particular emphasis placed by the impossibilists upon the inseparability of means and ends. If socialism is to be a society in which the conditions of life 'hitherto dominating humanity now pass under the dominion and control of humanity, which now for the first time becomes the real conscious master of nature, because and in so far as it becomes master of its own social organization',[32] then such a system is not to be created by minority imposition. The SPGB insists, therefore, that majority socialist consciousness is a prerequisite for socialism. The task of spreading socialist understanding and desire is not to be evaded, even though:

> the faint-hearted may shy away, aghast at the prospect of trying to convince the world's workers of the need for Socialism. It may seem an enormous task but there is no choice in the matter. Socialism . . . depends upon the conscious support of its people. Unless people understand Socialism and want it, they will never establish it.[33]

This socialist consciousness requires workers to experience 'a process of complete mental reconstruction. Years of thoroughly impregnated prejudices and attitudes towards social behaviour must be overcome . . . the whole ideology of capitalism will be rejected lock, stock and barrel.'[34] Images of The New Socialist Man come to mind – but socialists do need to think very carefully about this question of what it means to have achieved the necessary consciousness for social liberation. Two points can be made here about the SPGB and the recruitment of members – a subject about which there are more than a few myths. First, while it is true that the SPGB will not allow a person to join it until the applicant has convinced the branch applied to that she or he is a conscious socialist, this does not mean that the SPGB has set itself up as an intellectual elite into which only those well versed in Marxist scholarship may enter. The SPGB has good reason to ensure that only conscious socialists enter its ranks, for, once admitted, all members are equal and it would clearly not be in the interest of the Party to offer equality of power to those who are not able to demonstrate equality of basic socialist understanding. Second, the SPGB does not claim that socialist consciousness will come to dominate the working-class outlook simply, or even largely, as a result of the activity of socialists. As the Socialist Party of Australia puts it:

> if we hoped to achieve Socialism ONLY by our propaganda, the outlook would indeed be bad. But it is Capitalism itself, unable to solve crises, unemployment and poverty, engaging in horrifying wars, which is digging its own grave. Workers are learning by bitter experience and bloody sacrifice for interests not their own. They are learning very slowly. Our job is to shorten the time, to speed up the process.[35]

This contrasts with those who seek to substitute the party for the class or who see the party as a vanguard which must undertake alone the sectarian task of leading the witless masses forward into the next stage of history.

According to the SPGB, the revolution must be a democratic act. Political action must be taken by the conscious majority, without depending upon leaders:

> it is upon the working class that the working class must rely for their emancipation. Valuable work may be done by individuals, and this work may necessarily raise them to prominence, but it is not to individuals, either of the working class or of the capitalist class, that the toilers must look. The movement for freedom must be a working class move-

> ment. It must depend upon the working class vitality and intelligence and strength. Until the knowledge and experience of the working class are equal to the task of revolution there can be no emancipation for them.[36]

This brings us to the controversial question of *how* the independent, conscious, democratically organised working class will establish socialism. To say – as many superficial critics and vague advocates of the SPGB have – that the SPGB stands for 'socialism through parliament' or 'parliamentary socialism' is misleadingly incomplete. When Alex Anderson, the great orator of the SPGB's first years, was tackled by a syndicalist with the question, 'Does the SPGB really propose to establish socialism through the ballot box?', his reply was 'Yes, but most importantly we must win it through the brain box.' This linking of the conquest of state power with the concept of a consciously and democratically organised working-class majority, even if regarded as strategically incorrect, must be distinguished from the reformist parliamentarianism of those who, in the name of 'socialism', seek to enter parliament for other purposes than to express the majority mandate formally to abolish class rule. Engels rightly points out that the conquest of state power will be the final act of the working class;[37] the significance of such political action may be ignored by those within the 'anarchist tradition', but in the historical future it might be ignored at a tragic cost. Whatever may be thought of the SPGB's case for the working class, in the course of the socialist revolution, sending mandated delegates to parliament as well as organising industrially to keep production going, it is clearly those who insist that ballot boxes and parliaments can play no part in the establishment of socialism and assert that socialism can only be established via industrial organisation alone, who are being dogmatic and historically fetishised in their thinking about the revolution.

The non-dogmatic impossibilist position on the relationship between parliament and the socialist revolution was best summed up by William Morris:

> I believe that the Socialists will certainly send members to Parliament when they are strong enough to do so; in itself I see no harm in that, so long as it is understood that they go there as rebels and not as members of the governing

body prepared by passing palliative measures to keep 'Society' alive.[38]

STRENGTHS AND WEAKNESSES

In considering the strengths and weaknesses of the SPGB's impossibilism, one is forced to conclude that these characteristics are not politically separable: that which in one sense manifests itself as a strength appears from another angle as a weakness. Therefore, the temptation to list the 'good' and 'bad' points of impossibilism will be avoided and this chapter will conclude with three general observations which are intended to assist the readers in deciding the strengths and weaknesses of impossibilism.

The first feature which distinguishes the SPGB from other non-market socialist traditions considered in other chapters is its endurance over eighty years in a single organisation. In short, we are not just examining an intellectual tradition, but can observe the tradition as being contained within an essentially unchanged political party for a far longer period than any other concept of non-market socialism has survived organisationally. Thousands of workers in Britain have at some time been members of the SPGB and today, with a membership of over 600, the Party has quite tangible support from many more workers than that. If one turns to the *Socialist Standard* of 1904 one can read basically the same analysis of capitalism and statements about socialism as would be found in 1934 or 1984. There are some who would see such consistency as a strength and others who would regard such a record of unaltered social perception as a serious weakness. As an example of the former, the SPGB propagandist of the late 1970s, arguing against the reformism of the 'Right to Work' Campaign and pointing out that full employment cannot be created by governments and that even if it could such a condition amounts to no more than the right to be exploited, is able to argue with even greater credibility when he or she can point to the *Socialist Standard* editorial of November 1904 in which precisely the same argument is presented. Having existed long enough to have seen the possibilists' 'somethings now' burst to life and vanish into disillusion more times than the reformists care to remember, the SPGB has served as an observation post, charting the failed short-cuts of reformist history and storing them up for reference when the next possibilist rushes into the capitalist slaughter-house loaded with promises for the cattle.

The record of accurate prediction and sound analysis for which the SPGB can claim credit is an impressive one. Before 1906, when the Labour Party was founded, the reformist nature of that political movement was predicted. In 1914, when 'socialists' across the world succumbed to the temptation of national chauvinism and supported the imperialist war, the SPGB stood out in unqualified opposition to the war, producing at the time probably the finest anti-war manifesto ever to have been published in English.[39] In 1918, shortly after the Bolsheviks seized state power in Russia, the SPGB presented a Marxist analysis of the 'revolution' which foresaw its state capitalist outcome.[40] In the 1920s, the SPGB was virtually the only British contender for the theory of Marxism against its Leninist distorters within the Communist Party of Great Britain (CPGB). In 1926, the SPGB predicted that syndicalism, or trade-union militancy without conscious political action, was doomed to failure. In 1939, another world capitalist war was exposed as being nothing like a 'war for democracy' and was opposed[41] and, subsequently, the bogus socialism of Labour government nationalisation and welfare reform policies was predicted and charted.[42] It has been, in one sense, an impressive record of predicting historical failures: national liberation, CND, environmentalism, charities – the SPGB warned them all that, even on their own terms, these possibilist movements would end up faced with frustration.

A record of being right about the futility of other people's hopes and energetic actions has led to the conclusion on the part of many reformists that the SPGB is somehow opposed to improvements within capitalism. It would not be unfair to state that this misconception has been accepted by a few SPGBers themselves. A. E. Jacomb, writing in the October 1905 *Socialist Standard*, explains well the position of the impossibilist worker:

> I claim it as a fundamental truth that the object of every Socialist, as a Socialist, is the realisation of Socialism alone.

> As a husband, as a father, as a human animal, he has many other interests . . . but in his Socialist position none. As a man he may favour palliatives, the feeding and clothing and comforting of the destitute and suffering, but as a Socialist such matters are of interest only so far as they affect the attainment of his objective.

This distinction cannot be more than 'an abstract separation' (as Jacomb goes on to concede), but it is a necessary one for those less interested in short-term concessions than fundamental transformation. The SPGB states that it is opposed to reformism, but not to reforms.

The price of long-term persistence and validity of argument has had to be paid by the SPGB. Although many possibilists have a definite respect for the endurance and soundness of their impossibilist rivals, whom they would regard as being theoretically correct but practically unrealistic (an absurdly illogical conclusion), there are other possibilists who find few labels more contemptible than SPGB. This hostility was not unknown before the 1920s, when parties like the SDF and ILP devoted more words to attacking the SPGB than the Party's small size deserved. But it was in the 1920s, when the CPGB's Leninist mission began, that the organised attacks upon the SPGB commenced. By the 1930s, CPGB policy was to break up SPGB public meetings and CPGB members were actually instructed by their leaders not to speak to SPGBers lest they be tempted to believe the SPGB's 'propaganda' about the state capitalist tyranny of the Stalinist regime. When, in the 1940s, the West Ham branch of the SPGB invited the local CPGB to engage in a debate, they were told that 'The Communist Party has NO dealings with murderers, liars, renegades or assassins' who must be treated as 'vipers, to be destroyed'.[43] After the Second World War, CPGB union bureaucrats conducted a vicious campaign to oust from trade-union positions SPGBers who had refused to do their 'patriotic duty' in the war. The legacy of anti-SPGB slander has been slow to die, and it is common to meet Leninists even today who will repeat their intellectual predecessors' resentful attacks upon the party that would not fall in line with Stalinism; such prejudice is all the more tragic/comical when it is considered that many of the anti-impossibilist young Leninists of today are Trotskyists who are repeating – now that it is fashionable to do so – many of the arguments against Stalinism which were put by the SPGB half a century ago.

One does not want to paint a picture of the SPGB as the offended innocent, treated with hostility without cause. It must be remembered that the SPGB's Principles commit it 'to wage war against all other political parties, whether alleged labour or avowedly capitalist'.[44] This it has done without compromise and, at times, without making the necessary distinction between hostility of principle and of style. The SPGB has made clear that it is opposed to those so-called socialists, communists, Marxists and radicals who would appear to be its allies, and in so doing it has gained a reputation – largely, but not wholly undeserved – for a certain sectarianism. This latter characteristic has been stronger at different times in the Party's history, depending largely upon the outlooks of the most active organisers and propagandists in a particular period.

Another problem arising from the SPGB's longevity is that of credibility. After more than three-quarters of a century, a party calling upon the working class 'to muster under its banner to the end that a speedy termination may be wrought to the system'[45] is open to the accusation that, as the workers have not yet mustered and the termination has thus far been less than speedy, there must be something wrong with its policy. Of course, the reasonable historical answer to this is that lack of numerical support does not disprove the validity of a proposition. But, as the years have passed, cynics and empiricists have been able to contemplate with complacency the negative historical confirmation of their lack of hope for the SPGB's success.

The second concluding observation to be made about impossibilism, which can be seen either as a strength or a weakness, depending upon one's perspective, is that it has held tight to the basic tenets of Marxist theory. Indeed, two comments are made frequently about the SPGB: first, that if nothing else it possesses a fine knowledge of Marxism and plays a major role in spreading such knowledge; second, that the SPGB represents an orthodox, purist version of Marxism which has remained remarkably close to that which was revolutionary in the thinking of the theory's founders. The study of Marx's writings was frowned upon in Hyndman's

SDF – the ex-Etonian demagogue thought that SDF members would do better to study *his* books – and it was partly as a result of organising unauthorised Marxist economics classes that the young Jack Fitzgerald was hounded out of the SDF. From its inception the SPGB placed great emphasis upon the study and propagation of political economy. Indeed, it is the political link between the Marxist theory of value and profit and the revolutionary implication that class exploitation can *only* be ended by the abolition of wage labour which provided the most forceful theoretical justification of the SPGB's aim. SPGB propagandists, especially in the early years, placed great emphasis upon the concept of legalised robbery: the robber class and the robbed. Possibilists were forced to defend their palliative policies in terms of adjusting the operation of class robbery. In recent years, since many 'Marxists' have rejected economic determinism (a dogma which Marx and Engels were at pains to dismiss), it has become fashionable for 'Marxist humanists' to understate the significance of Marxist political economy. The SPGB has not followed this trend; it is still expected that official SPGB speakers should have a comprehensive knowledge of Marxist economic theory before they take the platform on behalf of the Party.

Whilst the SPGB has not failed to make clear those matters upon which it disagrees with Marx, some of which are far from peripheral,[46] its presentation of its ideas as Marxist has led to many difficulties. These are mainly the difficulties faced by any Marxist in the twentieth century who does not want to be associated with the opportunists and tyrants who claim to be following in the Marxist tradition. The extent to which modern Marxists can rescue themselves from such awkward intellectual associations depends to a great extent upon whether Leninism can be regarded as being part of, or in opposition to, the essential principles of Marxism. The impossibilists have devoted much energy to demonstrating the extent to which Marxism and Leninism are opposed to each other.[47] If such an interpretation is accepted, then the state ideologies of the modern 'communist' police states can be seen as Leninist, but not Marxist.

Like any theory, Marxism is open to dogmatic abuse, and, although impossibilist writers and speakers have tended generally to treat Marxist theory with a proper degree of critical reasoning, examples of Marxist dogmatism are certainly to be found sprinkled throughout the recorded history of impossibilist propaganda. But, despite the very real dangers of theoretical dogmatism, a distinction must be observed between the intellectual conviction which is a product of a theoretically defensible Marxist positivism, and the religious adjustment of social perception to fit in with dogma which is the product of a mind which has descended from reason to belief.

The third noteworthy point about the impossibilists – which is not unrelated to the origin of the SPGB within the English autodidactic tradition – is their tendency to argue in accordance with the strict standards of formal logic and empirical proof. Although such an admission would be regarded by certain European 'Marxists' as a confession of philosophical deficiency, impossibilists have always been suspicious of philosophical formulae and have never been impressed by the dialectical gymnastics of the fluid logicians, whose sophistication of thought is usually regarded as a refined front for evasion and confusion.[48] The impossibilists have always preferred clear-cut definitions, quotations, statistics, and logically comprehensible deductions to the methodological abstractions against which E. P. Thompson has written persuasively.[49]

Of course, it may be commented by critics that the price of impossibilist simplicity has been over-simplification. Faced with the choice between abstruse detail and simplification which may lack theoretical refinement, the impossibilists have erred in the right direction by opting in general for comprehensibility, even if it is occasionally at the expense of sophistication.

This concern for comprehensible propagandism is at the very root of the impossibilists' conception of their revolutionary mission. Always identifying their role within an activist, rather than a contemplative, context, the impossibilists have seen their purpose, in the words of William Morris, as being 'to make socialists'. And when all of the grandness of revolutionary rhetoric is brushed aside, it is, at the end of the day, the worker putting the case for the abolition of wage labour to her mates during the lunch break, the man on the soapbox who is cultivating new social visions in the imaginations of his listeners, the man who is known in his local pub as the fellow who is always talking about a world without money – it is these who are doing the real work of giving their fellow workers a taste for the impossible. When the taste turns into a hunger it will be time for those who need socialism to show, in ways which will ultimately be determined by them, that they possess the 'courage and strength to realise the impossible'.[50]

Notes

1. *Prolétaire*, 19 November 1881 (emphasis in the original).
2. Aaron Noland, *The Founding of the French Socialist Party, 1893–1905* (New York: Fertig, 1970) p. 13. I would not regard Guesde, Lafargue and the other French 'impossibilists' as impossibilists in the sense in which the term is used in this chapter.
3. *Rochdale Labour News*, October 1896.
4. Stephen Coleman, 'The Origin and Meaning of the Political Theory of Impossibilism', unpublished Ph.D. thesis (University of London, 1984). See also Chūshichi Tsuzuki, 'The Impossibilist Revolt in Britain', *International Review of Social History*, I (1956). Tsuzuki's article, whilst being very acceptable as a work of narrative scholarship, places less emphasis upon the intellectual conflict between possibilism and impossibilism than does my own study.
5. T. A Jackson, *Solo Trumpet* (London: Lawrence & Wishart, 1953) p. 66.
6. Circular statement issued by impossibilists within the SDF in May 1904. I possess a copy of this document.
7. *Socialist Standard*, September 1907.
8. See 'Who Are the Impossibilists?', *Socialist Standard*, November 1912.
9. Coleman, 1984, ch. 6. See also Stephen Coleman, 'What Can We Learn From William Morris?', *Journal of the William Morris Society*, VI (summer 1985) pp. 12–15.
10. H. M. Hyndman, *Further Reminiscences* (London: Macmillan, 1912) p. 2.
11. 'Art and Socialism', in *Collected Works of William Morris*, vol. XXIII (London: Longman, 1910–15) p. 208.
12. *Manifesto of the Socialist League*, reproduced in E. P. Thompson, *William Morris: Romantic to Revolutionary* (London: Merlin, 1977) appendix 1. Also reproduced in *Socialist Standard*, July 1985.
13. *True and False Society* (Socialist League, 1888) pp. 16–17.
14. 'The Society of the Future', in A. L. Morton, *Political Writings of William Morris* (London: Lawrence & Wishart, 1973) p. 201.
15. William Morris, *News From Nowhere* (London: Routledge, 1970) p. 31.
16. Ibid, p. 78 (emphases in the original).

17. Karl Mannheim, *Ideology and Utopia* (London: Routledge, 1936) pp. 176–7 (emphasis in the original).
18. See Morris's and E. Belfort Bax's *Notes on the Manifesto of the Socialist League*, in Thompson, 1977, p. 738.
19. See Adam Buick, 'William Morris and Incomplete Communism: a Critique of Paul Meier's Thesis', *Journal of the William Morris Society*, III (summer 1976) pp. 16–32.
20. See his *Critique of the Gotha Programme*, in Karl Marx and Frederick Engels, *Selected Works*, vol. III (Moscow: Progress, 1970) pp. 9–30; and proposed policies listed at the end of the second section of *The Communist Manifesto*, in Karl Marx and Frederick Engels, *Collected Works*, vol. VI (London: Lawrence & Wishart, 1976) p. 505.
21. *Socialism: Questions Most Frequently Asked and Their Answers* (New York: Socialist Labor Party, 1975) p. 20.
22. Marx and Engels, *Selected Works*, vol. III, p. 19.
23. See the articles by A. Buick and P. Lawrence in *The World Socialist*, 2 (autumn 1984).
24. V. I. Lenin, *Collected Works*, vol. XXXI (Moscow: Progress, 1966) pp. 77ff.
25. M. J. Panicker, *20th Century World Socialist or Communist Manifesto* (London: Panicker, 1951) p. 66.
26. *Socialism or Chaos* (Melbourne/Sydney: Socialist Party of Australia, no date) p. 19.
27. Philoren, *Money Must Go* (London: J. Phillips, 1943) p. 16.
28. *Socialist Standard*, April 1930. See also *Nationalisation or Socialism?* (London: Socialist Party of Great Britain, 1945).
29. *Questions of the Day* (London: Socialist Party of Great Britain, 1978) pp. 97–8.
30. *Socialist Principles Explained* (London: Socialist Party of Great Britain, 1975) p. 15.
31. *Socialist Standard*, February 1939.
32. Frederick Engels, *Anti-Dühring* (Peking: Foreign Languages Press, 1976) p. 366.
33. *The Case For Socialism* (London: Socialist Party of Great Britain, 1962) p. 42.
34. *Socialist Standard*, September 1980.
35. *Socialism or Chaos*, p. 35.
36. *The Socialist Party – Its Principles and Policy* (London: Socialist Party of Great Britain, 1934) pp. 22–3.
37. Engels, *Anti-Dühring*, p. 362.
38. Letter to Dr J. Glasse, 23 May 1887, in R. Page Arnot, *William Morris: the Man and the Myth* (London: Lawrence & Wishart, 1964) p. 82.
39. Reprinted in *The Socialist Party and War* (London: Socialist Party of Great Britain, 1970) pp. 60–2.
40. See *Socialist Standard*, August 1918. For detailed analysis of the SPGB's response to the Bolshevik *coup*, see Coleman, 1984. ch. 5.
41. The SPGB's statement on the Second World War is reprinted in *The Socialist Party and War*, pp. 62–4.

42. See *Beveridge Re-Organises Poverty* (London: Socialist Party of Great Britain, 1943), and *Family Allowances: a Socialist Analysis* (London: Socialist Party of Great Britain, 1943).
43. *Socialist Standard*, May 1943.
44. *Declaration of Principles*, clause 8.
45. Ibid, clause 8.
46. For example, the SPGB does not endorse Marx's ideas regarding struggles for national liberation, minimum reform programmes, labour vouchers, the lower stage of communism. On some of these points the SPGB does not reject what Marx advocated in his own time, but rejects their applicability to revolutionaries now; on other points the SPGB approaches social problems from a different angle from that adopted by Marx. There are, of course, other issues (not listed above) upon which the SPGB might appear to be at variance with Marx, but is in fact only disputing distortions of Marx's thinking.
47. See *Lenin Distorts Marx* (Victoria: Socialist Party of Canada, 1979).
48. See *The Socialist Party of Great Britain and Historical Materialism* (London: Socialist Party of Great Britain, 1975) ch. 7 on 'Dialectical Materialism', pp. 39–48.
49. E. P. Thompson, *The Poverty of Theory* (London: Merlin, 1978). See title essay.
50. A quotation from the anabaptist Thomas Müntzer in Mannheim, 1936, p. 192.

5 Council Communism

Mark Shipway

Council communism is a theory of working-class struggle and revolution which holds that the means that workers will use to fight capitalism, overthrow it, and establish and administer communist society, will be the workers' councils.

Historically, workers' councils (or 'soviets', from the Russian word for council) first arose in Russia in 1905. During that year, workers in many industrial areas engaged in mass strikes. In the absence of any widespread trade-union organisation, these strikes were organised by committees of delegates elected from the factory floor. Where workers of several trades or industries were on strike at the same time, delegates from the separate strike committees often met in central bodies to unify and coordinate the struggle. The most famous example of this was the St Petersburg Soviet, formed in October 1905. As well as agitating over economic issues, such as limitation of the length of the working day, the soviets also raised political demands, such as for the convocation of a Constituent Assembly.

The events in Russia in 1905 made a considerable impact on revolutionaries in Western Europe, and particularly in Germany. At this stage, however, the soviets were not yet regarded as the most important feature of the struggle; Anton Pannekoek, a leading theoretician of council communism whose writings will form the basis of this account, recalled later that the soviets were 'hardly noticed as a special phenomenon' at the time.[1] Instead, it was the mass strikes of 1905 which made the greatest impression, as typified by Rosa Luxemburg's famous account of 1905, which was titled *The Mass Strike*, and which contained only one fleeting reference to the soviets.[2]

For revolutionaries such as Pannekoek and Luxemburg on the 'left wing' of the German Social Democratic Party (SPD), the mass strike was one of the first signs of the emergence of new forms of organisation and struggle corresponding to new developments within capitalism. After the First World War this recognition was developed into a theory which saw the working class's use of parliament and trade unions as belonging to a period when capitalism was still an expanding system and workers were able to win substantial reforms. From around the turn of the century onwards, however, as capitalism entered the crisis which led to the First World War, it became increasingly difficult for workers to wrest any concessions from the ruling class other than through action on a mass scale. Furthermore, the end of capitalist expansion also opened up the prospect of a revolutionary overthrow of the system, and this was again a task to which new forms of mass action would be fitted better than the old parliamentary and trade-union methods.

When the workers' councils re-emerged in Russia following the February Revolution in 1917 they surpassed the point they had reached in 1905, setting themselves up as a rival to the authority of the state and then (or so it seemed at the time) seizing power themselves in the October Revolution. 'Now their importance was grasped by the workers of Western Europe', wrote Pannekoek.[3] In a pamphlet completed in July 1918, another prominent council communist, Herman Gorter, wrote of the soviets in Russia: 'The working class of the world has found in these Workers' Councils its organisation and its centralisation, its form and its expression, for the revolution and for the Socialist society.'[4]

Under the impact of the Russian Revolution, and the German Revolution the following year, various small revolutionary groups which had split from the SPD over its support for the First World War formed themselves into the Communist Party of Germany (KPD), voting by a majority to adopt anti-parliamentary and anti-trade-union positions at the founding congress in December 1918. When referring to this period, this anti-parliamentary and anti-trade-union majority can for convenience's sake be called 'left communists', since at the time their political views appeared to be a 'more extreme' version of the 'orthodoxy' by which they were defined, i.e. the Bolshevism of Lenin and the Third International.

Before long, however, the apparently tactical differences between the left communists and the Bolsheviks came to a head. During 1919 the left communist majority was forced out of the KPD by means of bureaucratic manoeuvring, and in April 1920 formed itself into the Communist Workers' Party of Germany (KAPD). The KAPD was one of the groups which Lenin attacked in his polemic against *'Left-Wing' Communism, an Infantile Disorder* (1920).[5]

Lenin's criticisms were answered immediately by Herman Gorter in a lengthy 'Open Letter to Comrade Lenin', written in the summer of 1920. Gorter had already expressed the basic premise of the 'Open Letter' in his 1918 work on *The World Revolution*, when he had argued that 'The conditions of the Western European Revolution, especially in England and Germany, are entirely unlike, and cannot be compared with, those of the Russian Revolution.'[6] Gorter argued that in Russia the working class had been able to ally with the peasantry to overthrow a weak ruling class. In Western Europe, on the other hand, the working class had no natural allies, and faced a very powerful ruling class. Therefore all tactics for the class struggle in Western Europe had to aim at increasing the power, autonomy and class consciousness of the workers. The tactics advocated by Lenin and the Third International – such as participation in parliament and in the trade unions, and alliances with Social Democratic Parties – came nowhere near to fulfilling such criteria. According to Gorter:

> As the Third International does not believe in the fact that in Western Europe the proletariat will stand alone, it neglects the mental development of this proletariat; which in every respect is deeply entangled in the bourgeois ideology as yet; and chooses tactics which leave the slavery and subjection to bourgeois ideas unmolested, intact.
>
> The Left Wing [by contrast] chooses its tactics in such a way that in the first place the mind of the worker is made free.[7]

At first, the KAPD, along with like-minded groups from other countries, fought for its perspectives within the Third International, believing that 'Whoever wishes to conduct the West-European revolution according to the tactics and by the road of the Russian revolution, is not qualified to conduct it.'[8] It met with no success in this struggle, however, and left the International in 1921 after the Third Congress.

Soon afterwards, a section of the KAPD (the so-called 'Essen Tendency') tried to set up a new, Fourth (Communist Workers') International. Given the reflux of the post-war revolutionary wave, such a venture was doomed to failure, but the Fourth International (or KAI) is still interesting in that the attempt to establish it had to be justified by a critique of the Third International, the Russian state, and the Russian Revolution.

The 'Manifesto of the Fourth Communist International' (written by Gorter in 1921) argued that the Russian Revolution had been a 'dual revolution': in the towns, a working-class, communist revolution against capitalism, and, in the countryside, a peasant, capitalist revolution against feudalism. This contradictory and antagonistic duality had been resolved in favour of peasant-capitalist interests in 1921, with the introduction of the New Economic Policy. Thenceforth the 'Soviet Government' had ceased to serve working-class interests; it had become a capitalist state. Insofar as the Third International was tied to the interests of the Russian state, it too had become a capitalist institution. Hence the need for the formation of a new workers' International.[9]

While Gorter was characterising the Russian Revolution as a 'dual revolution' – part communist, part capitalist – other left communists went further in their critique. In 1921, Pannekoek argued that 'the Russian revolution is a bourgeois revolution, like the French one of 1789'.[10] In time this view became predominant among the left communists. By 1923 Gorter seemed to have abandoned his 'dual revolution' thesis when he argued that 'even in their first, revolutionary, so-called communist stage, the Bolsheviks showed their bourgeois character'.[11] Another left communist, Otto Rühle, had come to the conclusion that the Russian Revolution had been a capitalist revolution even before Pannekoek or Gorter, and in 1924 he too wrote that the Russian Revolution had been 'the last in the line of the great bourgeois revolutions of Europe'.[12]

Thereafter the term 'left communism' became increasingly redundant. What had initially appeared to be disagreements over the tactics of the working-class revolution in Russia and Western Europe were now understood as fundamental differences between the methods of the *capitalist* revolution in Russia and the *communist* revolution in Western Europe.

Revolutionaries such as Gorter, Rühle and Pannekoek analysed the Russian Revolution as a 'bourgeois' revolution leading to the establishment of state capitalism. For the working class the lasting significance of the Russian Revolution did not lie in the type of society to which it had given rise, but in the forms of action used by the Russian workers during the revolution:

> Russia showed to the European and American workers, confined within reformist ideas and practice, first how an industrial working class by gigantic mass actions of wild strikes is able to undermine and destroy an obsolete state power; and second, how in such actions the strike committees develop into workers' councils, organs of fight and of self-management, acquiring political tasks and functions.[13]

Thus, through their central emphasis on the council form, those formerly styled 'left communists' came to be known as 'council communists'.

At the beginning of the 1920s the KAPD had claimed a membership in excess of 40 000. In close alliance were a further 200 000 workers in the revolutionary anti-trade-union 'factory organisations' under the umbrella of the General Workers' Union of Germany (AAUD). However, as is the case with any active communist organisations outside periods of revolutionary turmoil, these numbers steadily decreased throughout the 1920s, so that by the 1930s the council communists existed only as small, scattered propagandist groups, mainly in Germany and Holland. The Dutch Group of International Communists (GIC), which was formed in 1927, published the journal *Rätekorrespondenz* ('Council Correspondence'). This served as the vehicle for numerous important theoretical debates, many of which were taken up by the German revolutionary emigrés in the USA who had started publication of *International Council Correspondence* (later known as *Living Marxism* and then as *New Essays*) in 1934. This was edited by the ex-KAPD member Paul Mattick, and its contributors included Rühle, Pannekoek and Karl Korsch. The group in America had some contact with the longest-surviving British council communist organisation, the Anti-Parliamentary Communist Federation. The APCF (formed in 1921) published a succession of newspapers, the best and last of which was *Solidarity* (1938–44). During the Second World

War Anton Pannekoek wrote what is probably the best-known expression of council communist ideas, *Workers' Councils*, and he continued to contribute articles to the revolutionary press until his death in 1960. In the USA Paul Mattick published a number of books after the war, mainly concerned with a Marxist critique of bourgeois economics. His *Anti-Bolshevik Communism* (1978) collected together the fruits of a life-time's commitment to the revolutionary movement.[14]

THEORETICAL QUESTIONS

In examining the principal theoretical ideas of council communism, it is useful to bear in mind that council communism originally emerged *in opposition* to certain dominant trends within the existing workers' movement, in particular within Social Democracy and syndicalism. In fact, council communist ideas are perhaps most easily understood when approached from this angle.

In one sense, therefore, council comunism can be seen as a critique of the use of parliament and trade unions as weapons in the class struggle. In his early writings, Anton Pannekoek did not reject these outright. His text on *Tactical Differences Within the Workers' Movement* (1909) argued that parliamentary debates and propaganda during election campaigns could be used to 'enlighten the workers about their class situation'. Trade-union organisation could impart a sense of discipline, solidarity, and collective class consciousness. Agitation for reforms could also conceivably increase workers' class consciousness and organisational strength.[15] However, this assessment of the worth of parliament, trade unionism and reformist agitation indicates the point of view from which the council communists evaluated all forms of struggle, a point of view which Pannekoek summed up in *Workers' Councils*:

> Here is the criterion for every form of action, for tactics and methods of fight, for forms of organisation: do they enhance the power of the workers? For the present, but, still more essential, for the future, for the supreme goal of annihilating capitalism?[16]

As we have seen, in his polemic with Lenin, Herman Gorter had argued that all revolutionary tactics had to aim at increasing the power, autonomy and class consciousness of the workers. This was a point of view shared by Pannekoek, and it was on the basis of such criteria that council communists rejected the old methods of Social Democracy. Thus, in 1920 Pannekoek summed up his opposition to the use of parliament as follows:

> parliamentary activity is the paradigm of struggles in which only the leaders are actively involved and in which the masses themselves play a subordinate role. It consists in individual deputies carrying on the main battle; this is bound to arouse the illusion among the masses that others can do their fighting for them.
>
> . . . the tactical problem is how we are to eradicate the traditional bourgeois mentality which paralyses the strength of the proletarian masses; everything which lends new power to the received conceptions is harmful. The most tenacious and intractable element in this mentality is dependence upon leaders, whom the masses leave to determine general questions and to manage their class affairs. *Parliamentarianism inevitably tends to inhibit the autonomous activity by the masses that is necessary for revolution.*[17]

Before the First World War, Pannekoek had also criticised trade-union activity by putting exactly the same emphasis on class consciousness and autonomous activity. Within the unions, he argued:

> Success or failure appears to depend on the personal qualities of the leaders, on their strategic skill, on their ability to read a situation correctly; while the enthusiasm and experience of the masses themselves are not regarded as active factors.[18]

> Success of mass movements depends on their capacity for autonomous action, their unquenchable ardour for battle, and the boldness and initiative of the masses. But it is precisely these qualities, the primary condition of the struggle for freedom, that are repressed and annihilated by trade union discipline.[19]

As well as being a critique of parliamentary and trade-unionist methods from the point of view of working-class self-emancipation, council communism also emerged as an opposition to dominant ideas about what the overthrow of capitalism would involve, and how this would come about. In 1938 Pannekoek wrote:

> There are many who think of the proletarian revolution . . . as a series of consecutive phases: first, conquest of government and instalment of a new government, then expropriation of the capitalist class by law, and then a new organisation of the process of production.[20]

This had been the dominant conception within the Social Democratic Second International. Similarly schematic conceptions of revolution also prevailed within the syndicalist movement, which looked, for the most part, to the gradual building up of industrial unions within capitalism, the overthrow of the ruling class by the General Strike, and then the reorganisation of society by the unions.

Council communists rejected these ideas. In *Workers' Councils* Pannekoek wrote that 'victory will not be one event, finishing the fight and introducing a then following period of reconstruction',[21] nor would it involve a series of 'different consecutive occurrences'.[22] In Pannekoek's view:

> The revolution by which the working class will win mastery and freedom, is not a single event of limited duration. It is a process of organisation, of self-education, in which the workers gradually, now in progressing rise, then in steps and leaps, develop the force to vanquish the bourgeoisie, to destroy capitalism, and to build up their new system of collective production.[23]

This idea of revolution as a *process* is central to council communism, and it leads us directly to a consideration of council communist ideas concerning class consciousness and organisation, which Pannekoek described in 1909 as 'those two pillars of working class power'.[24]

In the council communists' view, revolution would involve the mass action of a vast majority of the working class. This was one of the principal points of divergence between the council communists and the Bolsheviks. The communist revolution, wrote Pannekoek in 1938:

> cannot be attained by an ignorant mass, confident followers of a party presenting itself as an expert leadership. It can be attained only if the workers themselves, the entire class, understand the conditions, ways and means of their fight; when every man knows, from his own judgement, what to do. They must, every man of them, act themselves, decide themselves, hence think out and know for themselves.[25]

As this passage illustrates very well, mass *action* is inseparable from mass *consciousness*, and the council communists continually emphasised that widespread class consciousness was one of the essential conditions of working-class self-emancipation. This is not to say, however, that the council communists thought that widespread class consciousness was an essential *pre*-condition of revolution, if this is taken to mean that a majority of the working class must be fully class conscious *before* any revolutionary action can be attempted. The emphasis in council communism tended towards the reverse of such a relationship between class consciousness and class action. As Pannekoek put it, the struggles of the workers 'are not so much the result as the starting point of their spiritual development'.[26] In keeping with their idea of revolution as a process, the council communists argued that *generalised, widespread* class consciousness could only be a product of workers' active engagement in the class struggle itself. In her account of the 1905 Russian Revolution, Rosa Luxemburg had argued that the 'high degree of political education, of class consciousness and organisation' which the working class needed if its struggles were to be successful could not be brought about 'by pamphlets and leaflets, but only by the living political school, by the fight and in the fight, in the continuous course of the revolution'.[27] Luxemburg's conception was shared by the council communists; in 1927 Pannekoek argued that class consciousness:

> is not learned from books, or through courses on theory and political formation, but through real life practice of the class struggle. It is true that prior to action, as well as after action, theory can be expressed in concepts that pre-

> sent organized knowledge; but, in order to develop in a real sense, this knowledge itself must be acquired in the hard school of experience, a harsh lived experience that shapes the mind in the full heat of combat . . . It is only through the practice of its struggles against capitalism . . . that the proletariat is transformed into a revolutionary class capable of conquering the capitalist system.[28]

In parallel with their view that widespread class consciousness would emerge from active mass involvement in the class struggle, rather than from 'simply converting people through propaganda to new political opinions',[29] the council communists also anticipated that working-class organisation, the second essential condition of the communist revolution, would arise in a similar way. The revolution could not be prepared in advance through gradually organising the working class in readiness for the single, decisive revolutionary act. In 1912 Anton Pannekoek criticised the attitude which held that revolution was 'an event in the future, a political apocalypse, and all we have to do meanwhile is prepare for the final show-down by gathering our strength and assembling and drilling our troops'.[30] Against this attitude he had put forward the view that:

> it is only by the struggle for power itself that the masses can be assembled, drilled and formed into an organisation capable of taking power.[31]

He repeated this view in *Workers' Councils*:

> The workers' forces are like an army that assembles during the battle! They must grow by the fight itself.[32]

Here Pannekoek's ideas echoed Rosa Luxemburg's formulation of the relationship between class struggle and organisation in *The Mass Strike*: 'the organisation does not supply the troops for the struggle, but the struggle, in an ever growing degree, supplies recruits for the organisation'.[33] In 1920 Pannekoek argued that mass revolutionary organisations (such as the 'One Big Union' or 'Industrial Unions' that syndicalists sought to create) could not be:

> set up within a still passive workforce in readiness for the revolutionary feeling of the workers to function within it

> in time to come: this new form of organisation can itself only be set up in the process of revolution, by workers making a revolutionary intervention.[34]

One example which Pannekoek used in *Workers' Councils* illustrates excellently the council communists' ideas about organisation. In the USA in the 1930s the presence of large numbers of unemployed (and therefore potential blackleg) workers meant that 'Any regular strike against wage cuttings was made impossible, because the shops after being left by the strikers, immediately would be flooded by the masses outside.' To overcome this problem, workers adopted the *occupation* tactic, i.e. going on strike, but remaining in the workplace. Workers also found that by occupying the workplace collectively, the striking workforce was no longer 'dispersed over the streets and homes . . . separated into loose individuals', and that strikes no longer had to be 'accompanied by a continuous fight with the police over the use of streets and rooms for meeting'. As Pannekoek pointed out, the occupation tactic, which almost as a by-product increased the solidarity and active participation of those on strike, was not planned consciously in advance of the actual struggles: 'It was not invented by theory, it arose spontaneously out of practical needs; theory can do no more than afterwards explain its causes and consequences.'[35] Again, there is a continuity here between the ideas of the council communists and of Rosa Luxemburg, for in 1904 Luxemburg had argued that 'fighting tactics' were not 'invented' by revolutionaries, but were:

> the result of a progressive series of great creative acts in the course of the experimenting and often elemental class struggle . . . the unconscious precedes the conscious, the logic of the objective historical process goes before the subjective logic of its spokesmen.[36]

Thus organisation and class consciousness are linked through a dialectical relationship. New forms of struggle and organisation arise spontaneously, in the sense that they are not planned consciously in advance, and they arise as a practical response to the problems faced by workers in the course of their struggles. Once these new forms have arisen, however, they can be made more widely known, and other groups of workers can begin to act on their example.

To sum up these ideas, from the council communist point of view the revolutionary process can be seen as one in which the working class continually adopts new ideas and new forms of organisation in response to the practical problems which confront it in the course of the class struggle. Once workers have taken up the fight against the attacks of the ruling class, the necessity to overcome the practical problems which crop up in the course of the fight pushes workers towards the realisation that existing forms of organisation are no longer adequate to their tasks, and that new forms have to be developed. In the course of an escalating struggle each practical step forward taken by the working class in serious pursuit of its demands leads in the direction of the overthrow of the existing system and the simultaneous reorganisation of society in the working class's own interests. As Pannekoek put it in 1920: 'without being communist by conviction, the masses are more and more following the path which communism shows them, for practical necessity is driving them in that direction'.[37]

This is not a unilinear process; advances and retreats follow one another. None the less, the underlying tendency is towards communism, if for no other reason than that reliance on outmoded ideas and forms of organisation invariably leads to defeats, whereas the adoption of new ideas and new forms brings successes. In his book, *Lenin as Philosopher* (1938), Pannekoek based this conception on a fundamental 'theory of knowledge':

> On the basis of his experiences man derives generalisations and rules, natural laws, on which his expectations are based. They are generally correct, as is witnessed by his survival. Sometimes, however, false conclusions may be drawn, with failure and destruction in their wake. Life is a continuous process of learning, adaptation, development. Practice is the unsparing test of the correctness of thinking.[38]

WORKERS' COUNCILS AND COMMUNISM

This basic account of council communism can be completed with a description of the role of the workers' councils within council communist theory. As was the case with the council communists' ideas on class consciousness and organisation, their emphasis on workers' councils is also understood best in the context of the central concept of revolution as a process. If revolution is a process, rather than a series of consecutive but separate events, then it follows that there must be a single organisational form which can be used by the working class throughout all phases of the struggle. In a slightly schematic way, it could be said that since communism is based on common ownership and democratic control of the means of production and distribution, the organisations which carry out the communist revolution must be ones which are suited to the realisation of this final goal. As Pannekoek wrote in 1938:

> Since the revolutionary class fight against the bourgeoisie and its organs is inseparable from the seizure of the productive apparatus by the workers and its application to production, the same organisation that unites the class for its fight also acts as the organisation of the new productive process.[39]

The organisations which the working class uses to fight against capitalism are therefore in a sense *pre-figurative* of the organisations which are used for the construction and administration of the new, communist society.

Council communists have commonly expected the workers' councils to emerge from mass strike movements where workers would take the conduct of their struggle into their own hands rather than leaving it up to existing organisations such as the trade unions. All strikers would meet in regular mass assemblies to discuss and organise the struggle, and to elect strike committees whose members would be delegates mandated by and answerable to the general assemblies and who could be recalled and replaced at any time. Where the strike centres were geographically dispersed, or as other sections of the working class joined the strike movement, delegates from the separate strike committees would meet in central bodies to unite and coordinate the struggle.

To the extent that it began to draw in wider and wider sections of the working class, the movement's demands would tend to outstrip their original starting-point, and tend towards the expression of the interests of the working class as a whole. At the same time, as a consequence of the interests of the entire working class being at stake, the general assemblies would be open to all those involved in the struggle – revolutionaries, families and relatives of strikers, inhabitants of the surrounding communities, the unemployed, and so on.

Within a fairly short space of time, the general assemblies and the local and central strike committees would be faced with tasks other than the pursuit of 'economic' demands. For example, they would perhaps have to publish bulletins or newspapers, in order to spread information, keep everyone fully informed about what was happening, and combat propaganda put out by the ruling class. They might also have to form militias in order to defend themselves against attacks from the armed forces of the ruling class, and to take the struggle onto the offensive. Thus through these and other necessary measures the strike committees would take on *political* functions, becoming in the process true workers' councils or soviets, organs of working-class power, rivalling the authority of the capitalist state.

Before long the workers would also be faced with the necessity of organising food and power supplies and other essential services, whose normal functioning would have been paralysed by the strike movement, in order to supply their own material needs. Where factories and workplaces were occupied by workers, to all intents and purposes the owning class would have been expropriated, and production and distribution would be restarted according to the needs of the workers. Here technical, social and political decisions would all be on the agenda: methods of production, what to produce and in what quantities, the basis of distribution in the event of shortages and so on. The workers would express their interests in all these matters by exactly the same means they had been using throughout the struggle: through their mass assemblies and committees of recallable delegates. In other words, 'The workers' councils growing up as organs of fight will at the same time be organs of reconstruction.'[40]

It is not hard to see the connections between this brief scenario and the theme of 'non-market socialism', for in the situation described above all the essential features of a non-market society are present, albeit in the most rudimentary, embryonic form: the property of the capitalist minority has been expropriated and is now the common possession of the workers; the uses to which the means of production shall be put are no longer decided by the capitalist minority but are determined by democratic discussion and decision-making in which all workers have an equal chance of participation; the fruits of production are distributed according to needs expressed by the workers, rather than according to capitalist considerations of exchange, profit and the market. It would be the birth of a moneyless society based on common ownership and democratic control of the world's resources, i.e. non-market socialism or communism (both of which terms mean the same thing).

COUNCIL COMMUNISM AND COUNCILLISM

The above sketch of the role of the workers' councils in the communist revolution is a suitable starting-point for an assessment of this current's strengths and weaknesses. Although the preceding account has been couched in speculative, 'would be' terms, this gives a misleading impression of council communism; council communists have always rooted their ideas firmly in the real experiences and struggles of the working class, and the councils themselves have arisen repeatedly in different periods and various circumstances during high-points of the class struggle. Although not always conforming in every exact detail to the rough outline sketched above – the councils of the German Revolution in 1918, for example, arose from the apparent collapse of state power following Germany's defeat in the war, rather than from a mass strike movement – on several occasions the actions of the working class have followed the pattern described.

Even outside of the pantheon of 'highpoints' – such as Russia 1905 and 1917, and Germany 1918 – there have been other times when workers' struggles have shown a tendency towards the emergence of the council form, even if they have often ultimately failed to realise their potential. The mass strikes of July–August 1980 in Poland are a case in point. This massive struggle was sparked off by the state's announcement of increases in food prices. The Polish workers responded with demands for large wage rises, and since they were well aware that the trade unions were a part of the state, they took control of their actions themselves, meeting in mass assemblies to elect mandated, recallable delegates. Rather than fighting separately, the workers extended and centralised their fight. In several regions inter-factory strike committees (MKS) were formed, constituted by delegates from scores of different workplaces. As well as negotiating with the state, the MKS also set up groups of workers to defend occupied shipyards and factories, and organised the supply of food, power, and other essential services to a limited extent; in other words, they took on some political and social functions beyond the scope of their 'economic' origins.

Council communism therefore has the definite merit of being based on something which actually exists and which cannot be eradicated, short of revolution: the continuing struggle within capitalism between the capitalist and working classes. It does not regard revolution as something which occurs on a totally different plane from, quite unconnected to, the everyday struggle of the workers. It sees communism as a potential lying within the everyday struggle, which will emerge from this very struggle. For the council communists, therefore, the 'communist movement' is not just the few organised groups of workers who are already class conscious; the 'communist movement' is also the 'movement towards communism', the real underlying tendency of workers' struggles within capitalism, which is indeed what gives rise to organised groups of revolutionaries in the first place.

According to council communist theory, the workers' councils are revolutionary organisations. They are not *permanent* mass organisations of the working class. They emerge at times of intense political, social or economic crisis when workers find themselves compelled to take matters into their own hands. Their sole purpose is to negate the authority of one class and install the power of another over every aspect of society. If they do not succeed in this task, the councils usually disappear with the defeat of the movement which produces them; in other words, when their source and lifeblood, the initiative, vitality and creativity of the working class, is drained away. Any attempt to maintain a permanent existence outside revolutionary periods changes the councils' nature: either they take on non-revolutionary functions (for example, negotiating with the ruling class 'on behalf of' the workers) or else they turn into small propagandist groups defending a political programme.

The potential for the emergence of workers' councils would thus seem to be tied closely to a contingent circumstance: the breakdown of the existing political, social or economic 'order'. In 1920 Pannekoek wrote that 'Economic collapse is the most powerful spur to revolution.'[41] At that time, very few revolutionaries did not sincerely believe (for obvious reasons) that capitalism was going through its death throes and would shortly collapse virtually of its own accord. Pannekoek himself did not hold this view, but the relative importance which he attached to conditions of economic breakdown would seem to be accurate. In the concept of revolution as a process, it is the workers' pursuit of their demands which almost inexorably leads them to take measures which are revolutionary. This may be credible during periods of capitalist crisis when it appears as if the working class can only satisfy its most basic demands by completely reorganising society. The Polish workers' struggle, for example, originated from the working class's protests about its inability to obtain one of its most basic material needs – food – but this original issue was soon outstripped as the struggle began to challenge wider and wider aspects of the existing society. However, such deep crises are not a permanent feature of capitalism. There are also periods of boom and relative prosperity for sections of the working class. During such periods there would not appear to be the same potential for the logic of events to lead in a revolutionary direction, for the capitalist system has a greater capacity to satisfy the material demands which workers place upon it. At such times, the conditions which would give rise to a revolutionary struggle and workers' councils would appear to be practically non-existent.

This leads on to the issue of how advocates of the workers' councils should organise themselves during periods when the emergence of workers' councils and revolution do not appear to be immediate prospects. This issue has been a subject of endless debate amongst groups of revolutionaries standing within the council communist tradition. Of the 'theorists' of council communism mentioned so far, Otto Rühle and Herman Gorter held diametrically opposed views on the role of the council communist 'party', while Pannekoek occupied an intermediate position.

Rühle's views on political parties seem to have been shaped decisively by the experience of the mass parliamentary parties of the Second International. His break with the SPD, which he had once represented in the Reichstag, led to an indiscriminate rejection of *all* political parties. In Rühle's view, all political parties were, by definition, 'bourgeois'. In 1924 he wrote that 'The concept of a party with a revolutionary character in the proletarian sense is nonsense.'[42] At the end of 1920, Rühle's sympathisers dissolved the sections of the KAPD to which they belonged into the local factory organisations (part of the AAUD). Rühle opposed the separation of economic and political organisation, and favoured a single, 'unitary' revolutionary workplace organisation. To this end he was influential in the formation of a breakaway from the AAUD, called the General Workers' Union of Germany – Unitary Organisation (AAUD-E) in 1921.

The tendency represented by Rühle was opposed vigorously by Gorter, who wrote that 'the factory organisation is not sufficient for the great majority of the proletariat to become conscious, for it to achieve freedom and victory'.[43] The class situation of workers in individual factories might prevent them from having a sufficiently broad over-view of the entire political situation. It was therefore vital for the most advanced and lucid revolutionary workers to form themselves into a separate communist political party, to act as 'the one clear and unflinching compass towards communism' and to 'show the masses the way in all situations, not only in words, but also in deeds'.[44] This party would not seek to seize power itself; Gorter believed strongly in the workers' capacity for self-emancipation, and, indeed, for the reasons he stated in his 'Open Letter' to Lenin, argued that there could be no revolution in Western Europe otherwise. As more and more workers took up communist ideas, the working class, the factory organisations and the party would merge into one entity, united on the same level of class consciousness, and capable of restructuring society.

Pannekoek seems to have vacillated between these two positions without ever settling on one or the other. This is perhaps not surprising given the great length of his period of involvement in revolutionary politics, and the changing objective circumstances in which he put forward his ideas. In 1920 Pannekoek supported a conception of the role of the party similar to Gorter's:

> The function of a revolutionary party lies in propagating clear understanding in advance, so that throughout the masses there will be elements who know what must be done and who are capable of judging the situations for themselves. And in the course of the revolution the party has to raise the programme, slogans and directives which the spontaneously acting masses recognise as correct because they find that they express their own aims in their most adequate form and hence achieve greater clarity of purpose; it is thus that the party comes to lead the struggle.[45]

In the 1930s, however, Pannekoek swung in the opposite direction, echoing Rühle's equation of all political parties with parties like the SPD: 'The very expression "revolutionary party" is a contradiction in terms.'[46] At this stage Pannekoek defined parties as organisations which sought power for themselves; they were therefore incompatible with working-class self-emancipation. Revolutionaries with similar ideas might come together to discuss and propagandise, and to 'enlighten' the workers through open debate with other groups, but these could not be called 'parties' in the 'old' sense of power-seeking organisations.[47]

Later still, in 1947, Pannekoek seemed to return to his original position, assigning the same functions to organised groups as he did in the 1930s, but upgrading their importance in relation to the actions of the working class as a whole:

> The workers' councils are the organs for practical action and fight of the working class; to the parties falls the task of the building up of its spiritual power. Their work forms an indispensable part in the self-liberation of the working class.[48]

Council communists have therefore put forward a number of different views on the party issue, ranging from Rühle's rejection of all parties as inherently 'bourgeois' to Gorter's emphasis on the party's vital role as 'the brain of the proletariat, its eye, its steersman'.[49] In general, however, the council communists' chief focus on the workers' own councils has assigned the political party to a less central role. The councils are neither created nor controlled by any party. They are the spontaneous and independent creation of the working class in which all workers participate on equal terms.

If this emphasis on working-class autonomy and spontaneity is taken to an absurd extreme, however, it can lead to two dangers: first, the denial of all necessity or reason for any political organisation distinct from the majority of the working class, and, second, the fetishisation of any organisational form created spontaneously and autonomously by the working class. In combination, these dangers amount to what has become known as 'councillism', i.e. an empty, *formalistic* emphasis on workers' councils which completely neglects the communist *content* of the council communist equation.

It is certainly safe to say that capitalism could not be overthrown, nor could a communist society be brought into being, *without* the self-organised activity of the vast majority of the working class. But this *in itself* is not a sufficient condition for the establishment of communism. If the class struggle escalated to a situation in which workers began to take the organisation of society into their own hands, it would seem reasonable to imagine that this would also be accompanied by a corresponding awareness, at the level of political consciousness, of the momentous implications of their actions. But while this may seem *likely*, there is sufficient evidence to suggest that it is far from *inevitable*. Although there is rarely any absolute separation between form and content in the struggles of the working class, neither are there any cast-iron guarantees of the unity of form and content.

It is conceivable that workers could spontaneously take over the means of production at a time of political, social or economic crisis, only to establish a form of self-managed capitalism. ('Councillists', in fact, see nothing wrong in this and have applauded the occasions when this actually appears to have happened.) The essential additional condition which must accompany widespread working-class self-organisation is, therefore, widespread communist consciousness. It is from this fact that the vital need arises for council communists to form political organisations of the type described by Gorter and the early Pannekoek, agitating and propagandising on the basis of a commitment to the goal of a non-market socialist society as the only working-class alternative to the existing worldwide capitalist system.

Council communist intervention in the struggles of the working class – participating in, supporting and publicising them, and endeavouring to deepen and extend them – should be informed by the perspective of a commitment to nothing less than the final goal of communism. This means, if needs be, defending the final goal even in opposition to the immediate actions and concerns of the working class, as the KAPD clearly understood:

> in the course of the revolution the masses make inevitable vacillations. The communist party, as the organisation of the most conscious elements, must itself strive not to succumb to these vacillations, but to put them right. Through the clarity and the principled nature of their slogans, their unity of words and deeds, their entry into the struggle, the correctness of their predictions, they must help the proletariat to quickly and completely overcome each vacillation. Through its entire activity the communist party must develop the class consciousness of the proletariat, even at the cost of being momentarily in opposition to the masses. Only thus will the party, in the course of the revolutionary struggle, win the trust of the masses, and accomplish a revolutionary education of the widest numbers.[50]

It was argued earlier that there is a dialectical relationship between organisation and class consciousness: that new forms of organisation do not arise as a result of shrewd forward planning, but once such new forms have arisen, their example can be spread and exert a conscious influence on the actions of workers in the struggles that take place afterwards. It is as a part of this dialectical process, as a link between the real struggles of the working class and its understanding of all the implications of these struggles, that organised groups of revolutionaries standing in the council communist tradition have their most positive and vital role to play.

Notes

1. Anton Pannekoek, *Workers' Councils* (1941–2) (Cambridge, Mass.: Root and Branch, 1970) p. 83.

2. See Rosa Luxemburg, *The Mass Strike, the Political Party and the Trade Unions* (1906) (London: Merlin, no date).
3. Pannekoek, *Workers' Councils*, p. 83.
4. Herman Gorter, *The World Revolution* (1918) (Glasgow: Socialist Information and Research Bureau (Scotland), 1920) p. 61.
5. V. I. Lenin, *Collected Works*, vol. XXXI (Moscow: Progress, 1966) pp. 17ff.
6. Gorter, *The World Revolution*, p. 51.
7. Herman Gorter, 'Open Letter to Comrade Lenin', *Workers' Dreadnought*, 11 June 1921. The 'Open Letter' (more commonly known nowadays as 'Reply to Lenin') was published in the *Workers' Dreadnought*, the newspaper of the left communists in Britain who were grouped around Sylvia Pankhurst, between 12 March and 11 June 1921.
8. Ibid, 4 June 1921.
9. The 'Manifesto of the Fourth Communist International' was published in the *Workers' Dreadnought* between 8 October and 10 December 1921.
10. Anton Pannekoek, 'Sovjet-Rusland en het West-Europeesche Kommunisme', in *De Nieuwe Tijd* (1921), translated in S. Bricianer, *Pannekoek and the Workers' Councils* (Saint Louis: Telos, 1978) p. 229.
11. Herman Gorter, *The Communist Workers' International* (1923) (London: 1977) p. 4.
12. Otto Rühle, *From the Bourgeois to the Proletarian Revolution* (1924) (Glasgow/London: Revolutionary Perspectives/Socialist Reproduction, 1974) p. 8.
13. Pannekoek, *Workers' Councils*, p. 86.
14. For a more detailed account of the German council communists during the 1920s and 1930s, and of the groups they influenced in other countries, see Denis Authier and Jean Barrot, *La Gauche communiste en Allemagne (1918–1921)* (Paris: Payot, 1976), especially pp. 189–216 and 221–30.
15. See Bricianer, 1978, pp. 73–117.
16. Pannekoek, *Workers' Councils*, p. 104.
17. Anton Pannekoek, *World Revolution and Communist Tactics* (1920), in D. A. Smart, *Pannekoek and Gorter's Marxism* (London: Pluto, 1978) pp. 110–11 (emphasis in the original).
18. Anton Pannekoek, *Tactical Differences Within the Workers' Movement*, in Bricianer, 1978, p. 105.
19. Anton Pannekoek, 'Gewerkschaftsdisziplin', *Bremer Burger-Zeitung* (18 October 1913), translated in Bricianer, 1978, p. 132.
20. Pannekoek, 'General Remarks on the Question of Organisation', in *Living Marxism*, IV:5 (November 1938), reproduced in Bricianer, 1978, p. 273.
21. Pannekoek, *Workers' Councils*, p. 54.
22. Ibid, p. 108.
23. Ibid, p. 91.
24. Pannekoek, *Tactical Differences Within the Workers' Movement*, in Bricianer, 1978, p. 87.
25. Anton Pannekoek, *Lenin As Philosopher* (1938) (London: Merlin, 1975) p. 103.

26. Pannekoek, *Workers' Councils*, p. 98.
27. Luxemburg, *The Mass Strike*, p. 32.
28. Anton Pannekoek, 'Prinzip und Taktik', *Proletarier*, 7–8 (1927), translated in Bricianer, 1978, pp. 241–2.
29. Pannekoek, *Workers' Councils*, p. 35.
30. Pannekoek, 'Marxist Theory and Revolutionary Tactics', in *Die Neue Zeit*, XXXI (1912), translated in Smart, 1978, p. 52.
31. Ibid, p. 52.
32. Pannekoek, *Workers' Councils*, p. 91.
33. Luxemburg, *The Mass Strike*, p. 62.
34. Pannekoek, *World Revolution and Communist Tactics*, in Smart, 1978, p. 116.
35. Pannekoek, *Workers' Councils*, p. 72.
36. Rosa Luxemburg, 'Organisational Questions of the Proletarian Revolution' (originally titled 'Organisational Questions of the Russian Social Democracy'), in *Leninism or Marxism* (Glasgow: Anti-Parliamentary Communist Federation, 1935) p. 14.
37. Pannekoek, *World Revolution and Communist Tactics*, in Smart, 1978, p. 95.
38. Pannekoek, *Lenin As Philosopher*, p. 17.
39. Pannekoek, 'General Remarks on the Question of Organisation', in Bricianer, 1978, p. 273.
40. Pannekoek, *Workers' Councils*, p. 54.
41. Pannekoek, *World Revolution and Communist Tactics*, in Smart, 1978, p. 94.
42. Rühle, *From the Bourgeois to the Proletarian Revolution*, p. 26.
43. Herman Gorter, *The Organisation of the Proletariat's Class Struggle* (1921), in Smart, 1978, p. 159.
44. KAPD, 'Theses on the Party' (July 1921), in *Revolutionary Perspectives*, 2 (no date) p. 72.
45. Pannekoek, *World Revolution and Communist Tactics*, in Smart, 1978, pp. 100–1.
46. Anton Pannekoek, 'Partei und Arbeiterklasse', *Rätekorrespondenz*, 15 (March 1936), translated in Bricianer, 1978, p. 265.
47. See Pannekoek, *Workers' Councils*, p. 101.
48. Anton Pannekoek, 'Five Theses on the Fight of the Working Class Against Capitalism', in *Southern Advocate for Workers' Councils* (May 1947), quoted in Bricianer, 1978, p. 267.
49. Gorter, *The Organisation of the Proletariat's Class Struggle*, in Smart, 1978, p. 163.
50. KAPD, 'Theses on the Party', in *Revolutionary Perspectives*, 2, pp. 72–3.

6 Bordigism

Adam Buick

In 1975 a pamphlet called *Un Monde sans argent: le communisme* (*A World Without Money: Communism*) was published in France. The authors argued for the immediate establishment of a moneyless, communist society:

> Communism is the negation of capitalism. A movement produced by the development and very success of the capitalist mode of production which will end by overthrowing it and giving birth to a new kind of society. In place of a world based on the wages system and commodities must come into being a world where human activity will never again take the form of wage labour and where the products of such activity will no longer be objects of commerce . . .
>
> Communism does not overthrow capital in order to restore commodities to their original state. Commodity exchange is a link and a progress. But it is a link between antagonistic parts. It will disappear without there being a return to barter, that primitive form of exchange. Mankind will no longer be divided into opposed groups or into enterprises. It will organise itself to plan and use its common heritage and to share out duties and enjoyments. The logic of sharing will replace the logic of exchange.
>
> Money will disappear. It is not a neutral instrument of measurement. It is the commodity in which all other commodities are reflected.
>
> Gold, silver and diamonds will no longer have any value apart from that arising from their own utility. Gold can be reserved, in accordance with Lenin's wish, for the construction of public lavatories.[1]

This pamphlet was published by a group which had been partly influenced by the situationists, as could be seen by their typically situationist name of The Friends of the 4 Million Young Workers. Above all, however, the group had been influenced in their ideas on a 'world without money' by the later writings of Amadeo Bordiga.

WHO WAS AMADEO BORDIGA?

Amadeo Bordiga (1889–1970) had been before the First World War an active and prominent member of the 'intransigent' wing of the Socialist Party of Italy (PSI). Bordiga and his comrades called themselves 'intransigents' because they opposed reformist trends within the PSI. Grappling with the problem of how to prevent a socialist party becoming reformist, Bordiga at first advocated expelling freemasons and other open reformists and the submission of the parliamentary group to the strict control of the party organisation outside parliament. Towards the end of the war he took this line of reasoning even further, arguing that, to avoid becoming reformist, the party should abstain from parliamentary activity altogether since it was seeking votes to get elected that obliged it to adapt itself to the reform-minded consciousness of the majority of workers. Eventually, Bordiga came to the view that the solution lay in the socialist party being an elite party, composed exclusively of socialists, which would not consider itself bound to take into account the views of the working class before taking action to try to achieve socialism. As this corresponded to a large extent to what Lenin and the Bolsheviks were saying (at least up until 1921), Bordiga became one of their partisans in the West.

He was present at the Second Congress of the Third International (Comintern) in Moscow in 1920, when Lenin convinced him to abandon his abstentionist position in the interests of founding a communist party in Italy. Thus when the Communist Party of Italy (PCI) was founded, as a split from the PSI, in January 1921 with Bordiga as its General Secretary, it did not advocate boycotting parliament and elections (although Bordiga himself always personally refused to be a parliamentary candidate). It did, however, remain thoroughly committed to the elitist conception of the party that Bordiga had developed.

For Bordiga the party was 'the social brain' of the working class whose task was not to seek majority support, but to concentrate on working for an armed insurrection, in the course of which it would seize power and then use it to abolish capitalism and impose a communist society by force. Bordiga identified 'dictatorship of the proletariat' and dictatorship of the party and argued that establishing its own dictatorship should be the party's immediate and direct aim.

This position was accepted by the majority of the members of the PCI of the time, but it was to bring them into conflict with the Comintern when in 1921 the latter adopted a new tactic: that of the 'united front' with reformist organisations to fight for reforms and even to form a 'workers' government'. Bordiga regarded this as a reversion to the failed tactics which the pre-war Social Democrats had adopted and which had led to them becoming reformist.

Out of a regard for discipline, Bordiga and his comrades (who became known as the 'Italian Left') accepted the Comintern decision but were in an increasingly difficult position. When Bordiga was arrested in February 1923 on a trumped-up charge by the new Mussolini government, he had to give up his post as General Secretary of the PCI but, on his acquittal later that year, he decided not to reclaim it, thus implicitly accepting that he was now an oppositionist. In 1924 the Left lost control of the PCI to a pro-Stalin group whose leader, Gramsci, became the Party's General Secretary in June. This loss of control was confirmed at the third Congress of the PCI, held in exile in Lyons in January 1926, at which the 'theses' drawn up by Bordiga and presented by the Left were rejected and those of the Stalinist leadership accepted.[2] At the end of 1926 Bordiga was again arrested by Mussolini and sent to prison for three years. He was formally expelled from the PCI in 1930 for 'Trotskyism'. On his release from prison he dropped out of all political activity until the fall of Mussolini in 1943.

The Italian Left, however, was not just a one-man show. In 1928 its members in exile in France and Belgium formed themselves into the 'Left Fraction of the Communist Party of Italy', which became in 1935 the 'Italian Fraction of the Communist Left'. This change of name was a reflection of the Italian Left's view that the PCI and the other Communist Parties had now become 'counter-revolutionary'. The 'Bordigists', as they became known, with their theory of the elite nature of the party and their opposition to any form of 'frontism', earned themselves the reputation in the 1930s of being a super-Leninist sect.

During this period they were not of any particular interest

to our theme of non-market socialism, since their views on post-capitalist society were the same as those of other Bolshevik groups: a period of 'dictatorship of the proletariat' (to be exercised by the party) during which money, wages, markets and other capitalist economic categories would be gradually phased out, ending in the establishment of an international, moneyless, marketless society in the distant future. As a matter of fact, they – like the Trotskyists – held that Russia at this time was a degenerate, or degenerating, 'Workers' State' rather than state capitalism. The Italian Left eventually came in the 1940s to recognise that Russia was state capitalist but those who argued this in the 1930s had to leave the group.[3]

With the fall of Mussolini in 1943, the Italian Left re-emerged in Italy itself, as the 'Internationalist Communist Party' (PCInt) which succeeded in attracting a wider audience than 'Left Communist' groups have normally done. Bordiga himself also became politically active again.

Generally speaking, too much importance should not be attached to individuals, but the fact is that Bordiga's reputation (founder-member and first General Secretary of the PCI, and member of the Executive Committee of the Comintern who had met, and argued with, Lenin, Trotsky, Zinoviev, Bukharin, Stalin and others) meant that his views carried more weight than others and, in relation to our theme of non-market socialism, it so happened that he put particular emphasis on the non-commercial nature of socialism in contrast to the commercial, buying and selling nature of capitalism. He frequently described capitalist society as a 'sewer' because of the effect it had on human behaviour, and it was clearly a gut reaction against capitalism's commercialism that was behind his political commitment.

Towards the end of the 1940s, as the wave of immediate post-war social unrest died down and the Italian Left returned to being a small sect, Bordiga came to argue that the period was no longer revolutionary and that all that revolutionaries could do in the circumstances was to preserve the revolutionary theory intact until the next revolutionary period came around. He thus set out consciously to 'restore', as he put it, revolutionary or communist or Marxist – he used all three terms interchangeably – theory. This involved him in writing and speaking on every aspect of theory – economics, the materialist conception of history, Russia, the national question and so on – but also on the nature of future society.

Before going on to examine in detail what Bordiga saw as being the essential features of future society, we need to complete our brief history of the Italian Left. Not all members of the PCInt agreed with Bordiga's analysis of the period. Some wanted to continue agitating rather than to concentrate on theorising and in 1952 a split occurred, the followers of Bordiga leaving to form the 'International Communist Party'. The names of the fortnightly publications of the two rival organisations, *Battaglia comunista* (Communist Battle) and *Programma comunista* (Communist Programme), rather neatly summed up the difference in their respective points of view.

Bordiga argued that 'the communist programme' had been laid down by Marx and Engels in 1848 and that the role of contemporary communists was simply to preserve and propagate it intact. Except on the key issues of the party and democracy, Bordiga did in fact stick very closely to the views of Marx and Engels, including their dubious positions such as support for national liberation movements and for the idea expressed in the *Communist Manifesto* for a period of state capitalist development between the capture of political power by the working class and the final establishment of socialism.[4] His writings on economics and history were strictly Marxist, although those on politics reflected, even more forcefully than previously, his earlier views on the elitist nature and role of the party. He also brought out well the fact that, for Marx and Engels, socialist society involved the disappearance of money, buying and selling, wages, the market and all other exchange categories.

Bordiga pointed out that Marx had distinguished *three* stages after the capture of political power by the working class – transition stage, lower stage of communism, higher stage of communism – the last two of which were *both* to be non-commercial and non-monetary:

> The following schema can serve as a re-capitulation of our difficult subject . . . :
> *Transition stage*: the proletariat has conquered power and must withdraw legal protection from the non-proletarian classes, precisely because it cannot 'abolish' them in one go.

This means that the proletarian state controls an economy of which a part, a decreasing part it is true, knows commercial distribution and even forms of private disposition of the product and the means of production (whether these be concentrated or scattered). Economy not yet socialist, a transitional economy.

Lower stage of communism: or, if you want, socialism. Society has already come to *dispose of* the products in *general* and allocates them to its members by means of a plan for 'rationing'. Exchange and money have ceased to perform this function. It cannot be conceded to Stalin that simple exchange without money although still in accordance with the law of value could be a perspective for arriving at communism: on the contrary that would mean a sort of relapse into the barter system. The allocation of products starts rather from the centre and takes place without any equivalent in exchange. Example: when a malaria epidemic breaks out, quinine is distributed free in the area concerned, but in the proportion of a single tube per inhabitant.

In this stage, apart from the obligation to work continuing, the recording of the labour time supplied and the certificate attesting this are necessary, i.e. the *famous* labour voucher so much discussed for a hundred years. The voucher cannot be accumulated and any attempt to do so will involve the loss of a given amount of labour without restitution of any equivalent. The law of value is buried (Engels: society no longer attributes a 'value' to products).

Higher stage of communism which can also without hesitation be called full socialism. The productivity of labour has become such that neither constraint nor rationing are any longer necessary (except for pathological cases) as a means of avoiding the waste of products and human energy. Freedom for all to take for consumption. Example: the pharmacies distribute quinine freely and without restriction.[5]

In other words, for Bordiga, both stages of socialist or communist society (sometimes distinguished as 'socialism' and 'communism') were characterised by the absence of money, the market, and so on, the difference between them being that in the first stage labour-time vouchers would be used to allocate goods to people, while in full socialism this could be abandoned in favour of full free access. This view distinguished Bordiga from other Leninists, and especially the Trotskyists, who tended (and still tend) to telescope the first two stages and so have money and the other exchange categories surviving into 'socialism'. Bordiga, as we shall see in the next section, would have none of this. No society in which money, buying and selling and the rest survived could be regarded as either socialist or communist; these exchange categories would die out before the socialist rather than the communist stage was reached.

BORDIGA'S 'DESCRIPTION OF COMMUNISM'

Since Bordiga's writings on the nature of future society are relatively unknown in the English language, in this section I shall summarise them using extensive quotations.[6]

Abolition of Property

Socialism, said Bordiga, involved:

> the negation of all property, or of *every subject of property* (private individual, associated individuals, state, nation, and even *society*) as of every object of property (the land. . . the instruments of labour in general and the products of labour). [1958][7]

This was because property was necessarily 'private' in the sense of excluding some – the non-owners – from the benefit of what was owned, which was precisely what socialism wanted to end:

> Even from the point of view of terminology, property can only be conceived of as being *private*. For land this is more obvious in view of the fact that the flagrant aspect of this institution is a fence surrounding an estate which cannot be crossed without the consent of the owner. Private property means that the non-owner is *deprived* of the possibility of going into it. Whoever exercises this right, whether a private person or a group, the character of 'deprivation' remains for all the others. [1958][8]

Hence:

> to define communism by 'state property' is a nonsense because the idea of 'social property' is itself one: when society as a whole becomes the master of its conditions of existence because it has ceased to be torn by internal antagonisms, it is not at all 'social property' that comes into being but the abolition of property as a fact and so as an idea. For how is property to be defined if not by the exclusion of the other from the use and enjoyment of the object of property? When there is no longer anyone to be excluded there is no longer any property nor any possible property-owners, 'society' less than any other. [1967–8][9]

The aim of socialism was to abolish property, not to change its form. Socialism was therefore to be defined not in terms of property in the means of production but in terms of social arrangements for using them:

> When the socialist formulas are correct the word property is not to be found but possession, taking possession of the means of production, more precisely exercise of the control or management of the means of production, of which we still have to determine the precise subject. [1958][10]

Bordiga went on to identify 'society' as this subject, so that he was in effect offering the following definition of socialism: a system of society based on the social control of the means of production.

Bordiga was adamant that socialism did not mean handing over control of the use – and thus effective ownership – of individual factories and other places of work either to the people working in them or to the people living in the area where those factories or places of work were situated. Commenting on a text by Marx, he wrote that socialist society was opposed:

> to the attribution of the means of production (the land in our case) to particular social groups: fractions or particular classes of national society, local groups or enterprise groups, professional or trade union categories. [1958][11]

Furthermore:

> The socialist programme insists that no branch of production should remain in the hands of one class only, *even if it is that of the producers*. Thus the land will not go to peasant associations, nor to the class of peasants, but to the whole of society. [1958][12]

Demands such as 'the factories for the workers', 'the mines for the miners' and other such schemes for 'workers' control' were not socialist demands, since a society in which they were realised would still be a property society in the sense that parts of the productive apparatus would be controlled by sections only of society to the exclusion of other sections. Socialism, Bordiga always insisted, meant the end of *all* sectional control over separate parts of the productive apparatus and the establishment of central social control over all the means of production.

So, for Bordiga, in a socialist society there would be no property whatsoever in the means of production, not just of individuals or of groups of individuals, but also not of groups of producers nor of local or national communities either. The means of production would not be owned at all, but would simply be there to be used by the human race for its survival and continuation in the best possible conditions.

Scientific Administration of Social Affairs

The abolition of property meant at the same time the abolition of social classes and of the state. With the abolition of property there would no longer be any group of people in a privileged position as a result of controlling land or instruments of production as their 'property', and there would be no need for any social organ of coercion to protect the property of the property holders and to uphold their rule in society. Social classes and the political state would eventually, in the course of a more or less long transition period, give way to 'the rational administration of human activities'. Thus Bordiga was able to write that 'if one wants to give a definition of the socialist economy, it is a stateless economy' [1956–7].[13] He also wrote that, with the establishment of socialism, social organisation would have changed 'from a social system of constraint on men (which it has been since prehistory) into a unitary and scientifically constructed administration of things and natural forces' [1951].[14]

Bordiga saw the relationship between the party and the working class under capitalism as analogous with that of the brain to the other parts of a biological organism. Similarly, he envisaged the relationship between the scientifically organised central administration and the rest of socialist society in much the same terms. Indeed, Bordiga saw the administrative organ of socialist society as the direct descendant of the party in capitalist society:

> When the international class war has been won and when states have *died out*, the party, which is born with the proletarian class and its doctrine, will not die out. In this distant time perhaps it will no longer be called a party, but it will live as the single organ, the 'brain' of a society freed from class forces. [1956–7][15]

> In the higher stage of communism, which will no longer know commodity production, nor money, nor nations, and which will also see the death of the state . . . the party . . . will still keep the role of depositary and propagator of the social doctrine giving a general vision of the development of the relations between human society and material nature. [1951][16]

Thus the scientifically organised central administration in socialism would be, in a very real sense for Bordiga – who was a firm partisan of the view that human society is best understood as being a kind of organism – the 'social brain', a specialised social organ charged with managing the general affairs of society. Though it would be acting in the interest of the social organism as a whole, it would not be elected by the individual members of socialist society, any more than the human brain is elected by the individual cells of the human body.

Quite apart from accepting this biological metaphor, Bordiga took the view that it would not be appropriate in socialism to have recourse to elections to fill administrative posts, nor to take social decisions by 'the counting of heads'. For him, administrative posts were best filled by those most capable of doing the job, not by the most popular; similarly, what was the best solution to a particular problem was something to be determined scientifically by experts in the field and not a matter of majority opinion to be settled by a vote.

What was important for Bordiga was not so much the personnel who would perform socialist administrative functions as the fact that there would need to be an administrative organ in socialism functioning as a social brain and that this organ would be organised on a 'scientific' rather than a 'democratic' basis.

Bordiga's conception of socialism was 'non-democratic' rather than 'undemocratic'. He was in effect defining socialism as not 'the democratic social control of the means of production by and in the interest of society as a whole', but simply as 'the social control of the means of production in the interest of society as a whole'.

End of the Enterprise, the Market and Money

The establishment of socialism, as the central social control of all the means of production, meant the end of the enterprise which, as a productive unit or group of separate productive units controlled by a single separate capital, Bordiga identified as the key economic institution of capitalism. In fact, the enterprise was the specific form which property took in capitalist society; it was a form of property in the sense that it represented the control of parts of the social productive apparatus, and of the products of those parts, by sections only of society.

Where control over the means of production was divided amongst enterprises, the links that had to be made between productive units to enable them to function as a productive system could only be commercial. Enterprises were linked to one another by contracts to buy each other's products. Thus the existence of enterprises implied the existence of buying and selling, of markets, of money and indeed of the whole commercial economy that was capitalism. Bordiga drew from his analysis of the enterprise-capitalist system the following conclusion:

Thus, the *socialist demand* proposes to overthrow not only

> *private property* law and economy, but at the same time the *market economy and the enterprise economy*.
>
> It is only when society is moving beyond these three features of present-day economy – private ownership of the products, monetary market, organisation of production by enterprises – that it will be possible to say that it is going towards socialism. [1948][17]

And he added:

> Capitalism exists as long as products are brought to the market or are in any case 'accounted' to the credit of the enterprise, considered as a distinct economic islet, even a very large one, while the remuneration of labour is debited to it. [1948][18]

The establishment of socialism, by centralising control over all the means of production into the hands of society, meant the abolition not only of enterprises but also of buying and selling, of money, of wages, of the market and of all the other categories of an exchange economy. On this point Bordiga was very clear and very consistent over the years:

> Modern commercial economy means monetary economy; thus the socialist anti-commercial demand involves equally the abolition of money as the means of exchange and also as the means of practical formation of capital. [1948][19]
>
> The capitalist mode of production . . . will have disappeared from the moment when there will no longer be any exchange values, nor commodities, i.e. when there will no longer be commercial exchange of consumer objects, nor any money. [1952][20]
>
> Socialism . . . is the economy which no longer knows markets, circulation, money. [1956–7][21]
>
> The communist revolution is the death of commercialism. [1958][22]
>
> Socialism . . . is the economy without exchange values (in the lower and higher stage). [1958][23]
>
> it will be a question of abolishing all exchange value and all production of values by labour. [1958][24]

By the same token, any society or scheme for social reconstruction which retained money, wages and the market could not be regarded as socialist:

> where I find exchange, competition, capital, money, etc., there I have the right to say: non-socialist, bourgeois economic form. [1959][25]

> a society based on wages paid in money is a non-communist, private property society, and let us add the corollary: even if there are no landowners or capital-owners. [1959][26]

> Wages are not the only positive economic phenomenon which allows us to state that the fall of the capitalist form has not yet been reached. We could express this same concept by saying that socialism does not yet exist when a *value* is attributed to *labour*; and it is the same when any other commodity is attributed an exchange value. [1959][27]

> where there is money, there is neither socialism nor communism, as there isn't, and by a long way, in Russia. [1959][28]

Bordiga was thus a vigorous critic of all forms of so-called 'market socialism', whether this took the form of the state replacing private capitalists but retaining the enterprise form (as in Russia) or of various schemes for 'workers' control' of enterprises. Since criticism of Russia as non-socialist and state capitalist is now widely accepted, I will only quote Bordiga on why 'workers' control' of enterprises is not socialist:

> The replacement of the boss and the bourgeois management by some 'factory council' elected as democratically as you want, in other words the replacement of the capitalist enterprise by an enterprise of a cooperative type, would not advance the necessary transformation of the economy by a single step. It is known that the attempts of workers' producer cooperatives in the last century, even if they did have the merit of showing that one could do without the social person of the capitalist, were a resounding failure because they were not able to stand up to the bourgeois competition. It would be no different if the competition took place no longer between bosses' enterprises and workers' cooperatives but between as many workers' cooperatives as there were enterprises. One of two things would happen:

> either the workers' cooperatives would try to operate other than as capitalist enterprises and as all the other conditions would remain bourgeois (links by the intermediary of the market) they would be swept aside; or, if they intended to survive, they would only be able to operate as capitalist enterprises with a money capital, wages, profits, a depreciation fund and capital investments, credit and interest etc. The competition between them would not be abolished, so neither would the system of commercial contracts, nor civil law and the state institution needed to uphold it. [1967–8][29]

Hence Bordiga's unambiguous conclusion:

> A system of commercial exchange between free and autonomous enterprises such as might be supported by cooperators, syndicalists, libertarians, has no historical possibility nor any socialist character. It is even a step backward compared with numerous sectors already organised on a general scale in the bourgeois epoch, as required by technology and the complexity of social life. Socialism, or communism, means that the whole of society is a single association of producers and consumers. [1952][30]

Planned Production of Useful Things

In socialism, said Bordiga, with the disappearance of money and exchange value, all that would be produced would be useful things directly as such:

> In Antiquity weavers produced the coat without producing the exchange value of the coat, adds Marx. And we, we add, absolutely sure: in communist society coats like everything else will be produced without producing exchange value. [1958][31]

This contrasts strikingly with capitalism:

> The bourgeois economy is a double economy. The bourgeois individual is not a man but a business. We want to destroy all businesses. We want to abolish the double economy in order to found the single economy which history already knew at the time when the caveman, with his hands as his only tool, went out to collect as many coconuts as he had companions in the cave. [1948][32]

In other words, capitalism is concerned with profit-and-loss accounting, as its aim is to produce monetary profits, but socialism would simply be concerned with producing what people need.

Deciding what people need was, for Bordiga, one of the tasks of the central administration, which, having decided this in the light of what a scientific assessment of the facts had showed was needed to ensure the survival of the human race in the best conditions, would then have to arrange for the goods to satisfy the needs of humankind to be produced and made available for individual human beings to consume.

To do this, the central administration would manage all the means of production – the whole already-socialised productive system that socialism would inherit from capitalism – as a single unit, drawing up a plan to use them rationally to produce what it had been decided was needed. In this sense Bordiga was an advocate of 'central planning', but, for him, these plans would be drawn up exclusively in physical terms (and not in both physical and monetary terms as in state capitalist Russia and similar countries):

> The basis of the future plans of the socialist economy . . . is that they are established outside the commercial atmosphere and the monetary means. Lenin called this kind of plan 'material plans', one could even say 'physical plans'. [1956–7][33]

> We affirm that the first socialist plan will be seen when its part expressed in the monetary unit is eliminated. [1956–7][34]

> a really socialist accounting, in other words with projects referring to physical quantities of objects and of material forces without mentioning monetary equivalents. [1956–7][35]

> Bukharin himself had said, quite correctly: 'at the moment that the means of production are socialised, the value form falls, and the only permitted accounting is that in nature (or physical)'. [1956–7][36]

> The rational relationship between man and nature will be born from the moment when these accounts and these calculations concerning projects are no longer done in *money*, but in physical and *human* magnitudes. [1963][37]

To those who said that such planning would be 'bureaucratic', Bordiga replied:

> The socialist economy kills bureaucracy not because it is applied from the base or from the centre, but because it is the first economy which goes beyond the muck of monetary accounting and of the commercial budget system. [1956–7][38]

To illustrate what he meant about plans in socialism being drawn up exclusively in physical quantities, Bordiga used the building industry as an example:

> One can give an idea of them by taking the example of a building project, accompanied by a forecast of 'needs for materials' and an idea of the number of work-days of an organised team, without making an 'estimate' but linking this work to the national plan concerning labour power, production and available goods. [1956–7][39]

In other words, plans in socialism would be drawn up as a list of the materials and labour needed to produce the various useful things that it had been decided were required to satisfy human needs.

Bordiga included labour, expressed as so many work-days, as one of the physical quantities in which the production plans of socialist society would be drawn up, but this was not the same as advocating the use of 'labour-time' as a general equivalent – a general measure of economic value – in place of money. Bordiga was in fact opposed to this. As far as he was concerned, it would not be necessary in socialism to evaluate all goods according to some universal unit of economic measurement; this was only necessary in societies where goods were exchanged, precisely as a means of establishing exchange ratios, but would not be needed in a society which only produced use-values directly as such:

> If there is accumulation in socialism, it will take the form of an accumulation of objects, of materials useful to human needs, and these will have no need to appear alternatively as money, nor to undergo the application of a 'moneymeter' allowing them to be measured and compared according to a 'general equivalent'. Thus these objects will no longer be *commodities* and will no longer be defined except by their

quantitative physical magnitude and by their qualitative nature, what the economists, and Marx also, for explanatory purposes, express by the term *use-value*. [1956–7][40]

In post-bourgeois society, therefore, it will not be a question of 'measuring value by labour-time', as fools believe, but of finishing altogether with the measurement of value. [1957][41]

In fact the whole revolutionary rebirth would collapse if each object were not to lose its character of being a commodity, and if labour were not to cease to be the measure of 'exchange value', another form which, at the same time as measurement by money, will have to die with the capitalist mode. [1958][42]

So Bordiga saw production in socialist society as being organised in accordance with a plan, established by the central administration, and drawn up and executed exclusively in physical quantities of useful things without having recourse to any general equivalent, neither money nor labour-time.

Bordiga expected that in socialism the level of production would eventually become relatively stable (which would make planning a matter of routine). It might even drop as compared with capitalism:

It can be established that the rhythms of accumulation in socialism, measured in material quantities like tonnes of steel and kilowatts of energy, will be slow and little above that of the growth of the population. Compared with developed capitalist societies, the rational planning of consumption in quantity and quality and the abolition of the enormous mass of anti-social consumption (from the cigarette to aircraft carriers) will probably bring about a long period of fall in the indexes of production and thus, if we take up the old terms, a disinvestment and a disaccumulation. [1956–7][43]

Among the other matters which Bordiga saw the central administration of world socialism having to plan for, in the interest of the human race as an animal species, was a stable population and a more even spread of the population throughout the globe (disappearance of the distinction between town and countryside).

Free Distribution and Social Consumption

In socialism, said Bordiga, the central administration, acting on behalf of and in the best interest of human society as a whole, would not only decide what should be produced; it would also decide how what had been produced should be used. Those at workplace level who had produced goods would thus have no say as to how those goods should be used – since if they did, this would mean they would have a property right over them and then society would not be socialism – but would immediately make them available to society to use as it decided:

> Society is immediately the owner of any product of labour supplied by each of its components, who have no right over what they have produced. [1956–7][44]

> The producers' associations of future society, whose membership will normally be renewed many times over the period of a man's life, will be associations having as their only aim the function, the act, the joy of producing. Not only to the extent that they will be following *a common rational plan* and to the extent that society will be *transformed into ONE producers' association* . . . , but above all to the extent that these technical, non-economic groupings of producers will place the whole of their product at the disposal of society and of its central plan for consumption. [1958][45]

The central administration would then make available for individual consumption the consumer goods that had been placed by their producers (or rather by those engaged in the last stage of their production) at its disposal:

> The administration, disposing at a given moment of all the goods that have been produced, retains when it comes to distribution the part which corresponds to general services and leaves the rest for daily individual consumption. [1956–7][46]

Only goods that could be consumed more or less rapidly would be made available for individual consumption; all other goods, including for instance houses, would remain social, to be used in accordance with the arrangements society would make for their use:

> In socialist society only the immediately consumable part of the social product which is due to him will be made available to the producer. [1956–7][47]

> we will speak about the worker having 'at his disposition' what he needs to provide for his 'immediate' consumption, immediate in the sense that consumer goods are not stocked but serve to cover in an extremely short period of time the whole range of his needs. [1956–7][48]

Thus individuals in socialism would not own consumer goods but would simply . . . consume them. As to the ideal of 'the family home', Bordiga regarded this as a stunted capitalist aspiration; indeed he denounced the family as a home-owning enterprise and capitalist consumption unit – a 'business' – which, like all other enterprises, would disappear in socialism, since all human beings, including all children, would have become members of a single human family. In socialism, houses would not be owned, but simply occupied by those who lived in them.

Naturally, there being no money, the goods which the central administration made available for individual consumption would be available for individuals to take freely without charge:

> In the socialist form production remains social, and thus there is no ownership by anyone of the instruments of production, including the land and fixed installations. In this society there will be no individual appropriation even for consumption; distribution will be social and for social purposes.
>
> Social consumption differs from individual consumption in that the physical attribution of consumer goods does not take place through the intermediary of commercial purchase and with the monetary means.
>
> When society satisfies all the needs of its members which do not conflict with the best interests of its development, *independently* of the greater or lesser contribution they have made to social labour, all personal property ceases and with it its measure, i.e. value and its symbol, money. [1958][49]

Bordiga preferred, as here, to speak of consumption being social in socialism rather than individual. This was because for him, although individuals would be free – at least in fully developed socialism – to choose which particular goods to take from the range of goods made available for individual consumption, they would not be free to choose which goods were made available. That would be a social decision made by the central administration in the light of what science indicated was best for the survival of the human race as an animal species. In other words, individuals would be consuming not so much for their own personal benefit as for the benefit of the whole species.

The point Bordiga was trying to make here was that not even in full socialism would individuals be able to consume whatever they might feel they wanted to; they would only be able to consume whatever society had decided should be available for individual consumption. Thus, to use an example Bordiga gave, people would only be able to smoke cigarettes if socialist society decided to produce them (which Bordiga thought unlikely); or people would only be able to visit the moon if socialist society decided to devote resources to provide facilities for all who wanted to go there.

SOCIALISM?

The description of future society given here evidently earns Bordiga a place amongst those advocating a non-market society to replace capitalism, but, in view of the 'non-democratic' character of the administrative structure which he envisaged future society as having, the question of the extent to which it can be regarded as socialist must be seriously faced.

If democracy is simply defined as *political* democracy, that is, as a form of state, then clearly socialism, as a stateless society, would be non-democratic. But Bordiga was saying much more than this. He was saying that in socialism the mass of the people would not participate at all in the administration of social affairs; there would be no elections, nor would decisions be made by majority vote. On the contrary, all important social decisions would be made by a central administration which would be the direct successor of the vanguard party.

Bordiga does not seem to have realised the extent to which restricting decision-making to a minority within society, even to an elite of well-meaning social and scientific experts, conflicted with his definition of socialism as the abolition of property. For property, as Bordiga well realised, is a social fact, not a legal state; it exists when control over the use of something is *de facto* in the hands of some individual or some group to the exclusion of all other individuals and groups. Clearly, this situation would still apply in Bordiga's socialism, with the elite central administration as the owners (*de facto* controllers) of all the means of production, since the power to decide how to use them would be exclusively theirs.

If, however, we ignore this aspect of his views, then Bordiga can be said to have given a very clear description of socialist/communist society. In particular, he demonstrated with great clarity:

(a) that it would not be based on state (or nationalised), or even on common (or social), property, but on the complete absence of any exclusive use-controlling rights over the means of production and their products; and
(b) that it would involve the complete disappearance of buying and selling, of money and monetary calculation, of wages and of all other exchange categories, including enterprises as autonomous economic and accounting units.

The technocratic aspects of Bordiga's 'description of communism' were ignored by most of those influenced by him, including to a large extent the members of the group with which he was associated (the International Communist Party). The important point is that, thanks in part to the writings of Bordiga, the realisation that socialism is neither the state ownership nor the workers' control (through factory committees, workers' councils and the like) of enterprises engaged in profit-and-loss accounting (whether in money or labour-time) has been encouraged. Conversely, the idea that socialism must be a moneyless, wageless society has been, and still is, propagated by a number of groups and individuals influenced by Bordiga's views on this, particularly in France, Italy and Spain.

The fact that the idea of such a society as the only solution to the problems currently facing humankind in general, and wage- and salary-earners in particular, should have arisen, and be propagated, in these countries quite independently of the anglo-saxon groups putting forward this idea (which are discussed in Chapter 4), is confirmation of the view that the spread of non-market socialist ideas does not depend exclusively on the efforts of one or other particular socialist sect but is generated by capitalism itself.

Notes

1. *Un Monde sans argent: le communisme* (Paris: Les Amis de 4 Millions de Jeunes Travailleurs, 1975) pp. 1 and 8.
2. For this period of Bordiga's political activity, see Andreina De Clementi, *Amadeo Bordiga* (Turin: Einaudi, 1971). In English there is Earlene Craver, 'The Rediscovery of Amadeo Bordiga', *Survey*, XX (spring/summer 1974). Otherwise Bordiga is just a footnote reference in the many books on Gramsci. See also 'Bordiga and the Idea of Socialism', *Socialist Standard*, February 1982, and 'Notes on Trotsky, Pannekoek and Bordiga', in Jean Barrot and François Martin, *Eclipse and Re-emergence of the Communist Movement* (Detroit: Black and Red, 1974) pp. 119–31.
3. *Bilan*, the monthly theoretical bulletin of the Italian Left during the period 1933–8, continually referred to Russia as 'a degenerate Workers' State'. For a 'state capitalist' breakaway which occurred in 1933, see *La Gauche communiste d'Italie* (Brussels: International Communist Current, 1983) p. 84. This pamphlet, based on a university thesis by one of the Belgian members of the ICC, is a good and generally objective history of the Italian Left.
4. Karl Marx and Frederick Engels, *Collected Works*, vol. VI (London: Lawrence & Wishart, 1976) pp. 504–5.
5. Amadeo Bordiga, 'Dialogue avec Staline' (1952), quoted in Jacques Camatte, *Bordiga et la passion du communisme: Textes essentiels de Bordiga et repères biographiques* (Paris: Spartacus, 1974) pp. 18–19 (emphases in the original).
6. Translated from the French, since French translations of Bordiga's writings are more readily available to me than the Italian originals. The date references after quotations refer to the Italian original, not the French translation.
7. Amadeo Bordiga, 'Le Programme révolutionnaire de la société communiste élimine toute forme de propriété de la terre, des installations productives et des produits du travail', in Camatte, 1974, p. 54 (emphases in the original).

8. Ibid, p. 54 (emphases in the original).
9. *Bilan d'une révolution.* Special Number of *Programme Communiste*, 40-41-42 (Paris: International Communist Party, October 1967–June 1968) p. 78.
10. Bordiga, 'Le Programme révolutionnaire', in Camatte, 1974, pp. 46–7.
11. Ibid, p. 60.
12. Ibid, p. 50 (emphasis in the original).
13. Amadeo Bordiga, *Structure économique et sociale de la Russie d'aujourd'hui* (Paris: Editions de l'Oubli, 1975) p. 310.
14. Amadeo Bordiga, 'Dictature prolétarienne et parti de classe', in *Textes fondamentaux de la gauche communiste* in *La Révolution Communiste*, 3 (Brussels: 1984) pp. 67–8.
15. Bordiga, 1975, p. 95 (emphasis in the original).
16. Bordiga, 'Dictature prolétarienne', in *Textes fondamentaux*, 1984, p. 70.
17. Extract from Amadeo Bordiga, *Propriété et Capital* (1948), in *Socialisme prolétarien contre socialisme petit-bourgeois*. Supplement to *Le Prolétaire*, 312 (Paris: 1980) p. 24.
18. Ibid, p. 24.
19. Ibid, p. 22.
20. Amadeo Bordiga, *Russie et révolution dans la théorie marxiste* (Paris: Spartacus, 1978) p. 140.
21. Bordiga, 1975, p. 315.
22. Bordiga, 'Le Programme révolutionnaire', in Camatte, 1974, p. 69.
23. Amadeo Bordiga, 'Le Contenu original du programme communiste est l'abolition de l'individu comme sujet économique, détenteur de droits et acteur de l'histoire humaine', in Camatte, 1974, p. 104.
24. Ibid, p. 105.
25. Amadeo Bordiga, 'Commentaires des manuscrits de 1844', in Camatte, 1974, p. 134.
26. Ibid, p. 130.
27. Ibid, p. 134 (emphases in the original).
28. Amadeo Bordiga, 'Tables immuables de la théorie communiste de parti', in Camatte, 1974, p. 179.
29. *Bilan d'une révolution*, 1967–8, pp. 75–6.
30. Bordiga, 1978, p. 172.
31. Bordiga, 'Le Contenu original du programme communiste', in Camatte, 1974, p. 104.
32. Bordiga, 'Socialisme prolétarien', p. 24.
33. Bordiga, 1975, p. 202.
34. Ibid, p. 203.
35. Ibid, p. 140.
36. Ibid, p. 205.
37. Amadeo Bordiga, 'La Légende du Piave', quoted in Camatte, 1974, p. 23 (emphases in the original).
38. Bordiga, 1975, p. 340.
39. Ibid, p. 140.
40. Ibid, pp. 191–2 (emphases in the original).

41. Amadeo Bordiga in *Il programma comunista*, 20 (1957), quoted in Jacques Camatte, *Capital et Gemeinwesen* (Paris: Spartacus, 1976) p. 213.
42. Bordiga, 'Le Programme révolutionnaire', in Camatte, 1974, pp. 70–1.
43. Bordiga, 1975, p. 192.
44. Ibid, p. 166.
45. Bordiga, 'Le Contenu original du programme communiste', in Camatte, 1974, pp. 87–8 (emphases in the original).
46. Bordiga, 1975, p. 318.
47. Ibid, p. 294.
48. Ibid, p. 291.
49. Bordiga, 'Le Contenu original du programme communiste', in Camatte, 1974, pp. 79–80 (emphasis in the original).

7 Situationism

Mark Shipway

The various currents which constitute the 'thin red line' of non-market socialism have arisen at different periods in history and in different parts of the world. These seemingly diverse groups are united, none the less, by having all worked out similar analyses of the problems posed by capitalist society, and by having all reached the same conclusions about the type of society which they envisage would have to replace capitalism. The idea of a non-market society is a persistent and recurrent response to capitalism on the part of wage labourers. Moreover, as is shown by the origins and development of the current discussed in this chapter, the non-market alternative is quite capable of arising from seemingly improbable sources, and under apparently unfamiliar guises.

ORIGINS AND HISTORY

The Situationist International (SI) was formed in July 1957 after the unification of three small artistic avant-garde groups, including the Lettrist International around Guy Debord and the Movement for an Imaginist Bauhaus around Asger Jorn. One year later (June 1958) the SI published the first issue of a journal, *Internationale Situationniste*, in Paris. In all, twelve issues of the journal appeared, at irregular intervals, over the next eleven years.

The contents of the first few issues reflected the SI's origins in the cultural avant-garde movement, with articles on cinema, art, literature, 'urbanism' (town planning) and related subjects. An article in *Internationale Situationniste*, 9 (1964) later recalled 'the fantasies left over from the old artistic milieu' in 'our first publications',[1] while in 1968 Guy Debord wrote that there had been two 'periods' in the history of the SI, 'if the 1957–1962 activity that centred around the supersession of art is counted as the first'.[2]

The 'supersession of art' which preoccupied the SI in its earliest years meant the supersession of art as a specialised activity separated from most people's everyday lives. Within capitalism, the SI's argument ran, most people's creativity is alienated, and appropriated by an exclusive category of specialists – 'artists'. As a consequence, society is divided into actors and audience, creators and spectators. This was an idea which was preserved throughout the SI's lifetime, although it came to be applied far beyond the realm of culture, as part of a critique of *all* aspects of capitalist society.

During 1960–1 most of the pure and simple 'artistic' elements resigned or were expelled from the SI, so that from 1962 onwards it became clear that the SI had evolved from a group of experimental artists into a revolutionary organisation which can be more readily recognised and understood as a strand in the thin red line of non-market socialism.

The watershed between these two phases in the SI's activities is best represented by an article titled 'The Bad Days Will End', published in 1962. Here, the SI set itself the project of 'rediscover[ing] the history' of 'the first workers' movement', i.e. from 'the first linking up of communist groups that Marx and his friends organised from Brussels in 1845' through to 'the failure of the Spanish revolution . . . after the Barcelona May days of 1937'. Not only Marxism, but also 'the anarchist positions in the First International, Blanquism, Luxemburgism, the council movement in Germany and Spain, Kronstadt, the Makhnovists etc.' were to be reexamined and reassessed 'with the aim of contributing toward the formation of a new revolutionary movement', the basis of which would be 'the new proletariat' in 'the industrially advanced countries'.[3]

At no stage was the SI ever a large organisation, at least in terms of numbers. Only 70 individuals ever became members during the fifteen years of its existence, and never more than ten or twenty belonged to the group at any one time. Frequent 'exclusions' were used as a means of preserving the group's theoretical coherence, while aspiring members were just as regularly turned away – the SI did not want 'disciples' any more than it wanted to become a 'leadership'. However, over the period 1966–8 the SI showed, in the words of its own assessment, 'what can be done in the first stage of reappearance of the revolutionary proletarian movement by a few basically coherent individuals'.[4]

During the summer of 1966 the SI was approached on behalf of six Strasbourg University students who had been elected to office of the local branch of the National Union of French Students. On the initiative of the SI, a project was devised which involved the use of large sums of students' union funds to publish 10 000 copies of a text drafted by Mustapha Khayati, called *On the Poverty of Student Life*. The distribution of this pamphlet at the University's official opening ceremony was preceded by the disruption of lectures and widespread flyposting of André Bertrand's comic-strip poster, 'The Return of the Durruti Column'. In condemning these actions, a local magistrate inadvertently caught the essence of the SI's interventions:

> Rejecting all morality and restraint, these cynics do not hesitate to commend theft, the destruction of scholarship, the abolition of work, total subversion and a world-wide proletarian revolution with 'unlicensed pleasure' as its only goal.[5]

The scandalised reaction of 'the holy alliance of the bourgeois, the Stalinists and the priests',[6] the judicial repression launched against the officers of the students' union in December 1966, and the widespread translation and publication of Khayati's text outside France during the following months, at last assured the SI a notoriety and influence out of all proportion to its size. Beyond the relatively tiny nucleus of 'card-carrying' members, many times that number came to consider themselves as situationists and began to propagate the SI's ideas.

Alongside lampoons such as the 'Strasbourg Scandal', members of the SI also continued to deepen their theoretical analysis of capitalism and its revolutionary alternative. The two most developed expressions of situationist theory were published at the end of 1967: Guy Debord's 221 theses on *The Society of the Spectacle* and Raoul Vaneigem's *Traité de savoir-vivre à l'usage des jeunes générations* (known in its English-language translations as *The Revolution of Everyday Life*).

It was during the mass strikes, factory occupations and student revolts of May–June 1968 in France that the SI reached the height of its fame. According to René Viénet's account:

> the positions or the phrases of the two books of Situationist theory which had appeared in the last weeks of 1967 [i.e. Debord's and Vaneigem's] were written on the walls of Paris and several provincial cities by the most advanced elements of the May uprising. The greater part of these theses took up a greater part of these walls.[7]

The SI viewed the 1968 'uprising' as a dramatic affirmation of the truth of the theories which it had been developing and propagating during the previous few years. Members of the SI themselves, along with the Nanterre 'Enragés' group with whom they had been cooperating since February 1968, participated in the Occupation Committee elected by the general assembly of the Sorbonne University from 14 to 17 May. When the vitality of the general assembly's 'direct democracy' was sapped by 'the steady encroachment of the various bureaucratic leftist sects'[8] the situationists and Enragés resigned and immediately formed a 'Council for the Continuation of Occupations' (CMDO). The core of the CMDO consisted of 'About 40 people . . . ten Situationists and Enragés (among them Debord, Khayati, Riesel and Vaneigem) and as many from the workers, the high school students or "students", and other councillists without specific social functions.'[9] The CMDO was active until 15 June 1968, when it decided to dissolve as a consequence of the ebbing of the actual occupation movement it had existed to support.

The SI's account and analysis of the events of May–June 1968 – 'The Beginning of an Era' – appeared in *Internationale Situationniste* 12, published in September 1969. However, the 'beginning of an era' for the 'new revolutionary movement' turned out to be the end of an era for the SI. No further issues of the *Internationale Situationniste* were published; 'The organisation itself broke up amidst bitter tactical wrangling over 1969–1970.'[10] There were conflicts over what direction the group should take next, and also over how these conflicts could be expressed through the group's internal organisation. Raoul Vaneigem, for instance, resigned from the SI in 1970, later drawing attention to the problem of 'the perpetual re-emergence within [the SI] of the relationships characteristic of the dominant world outside'.[11] The group was eventually dissolved formally in 1972, although many of its ex-members continued to be active politically afterwards. By 1972 many of the SI's ideas and tactics had also been taken up by groups and individuals in countries throughout the world.[12] The following account, however, concentrates on situationist ideas as they were developed by the SI itself during the period 1957–72.

PRINCIPAL THEORETICAL IDEAS

The key concept in situationist theory was that of the *spectacle*, as already mentioned briefly in the description of the SI's ideas about the 'supersession of art'. With its connotations of estrangement, separation and passive contemplation, the concept of the spectacle underlay the situationists' critique of all aspects of modern capitalist society.

In certain aspects, the situationists' use of the concept of the spectacle was a fairly straightforward restatement of Marx's writings on alienation in the *Economic and Philosophic Manuscripts of 1844*. This is particularly obvious in certain passages of Debord's book, *The Society of the Spectacle*. Because private property relations underlie the relations of production within capitalism, the worker is separated (or alienated) from the objects which he or she produces, from the activity which goes into production, and from his or her fellow producers. As Debord put it, 'With the generalised separation of the worker and his products, every unitary view of accomplished activity and all direct personal communication among producers are lost.'[13] The goods which the worker produces confront him or her as apparently independent, alien powers. Moreover, it is not just this or that object which appears alien to the producer; all objects are alien and so, in sum, form a complete world which is separate and alien. In effect, every moment spent in production is a moment spent creating a world from which the producers are ever more separated. Debord again:

> The worker does not produce himself; he produces an independent power. The *success* of this production, its abun-

> dance, returns to the producer as an *abundance of dispossession*. All the time and space of his world become *foreign* to him with the accumulation of his alienated products . . . Separated from his product, man himself produces all the details of his world with ever increasing power, and thus finds himself ever more separated from his world.[14]

The situationists also had many trenchant criticisms to make of the nature of productive activity within capitalism. With the 'incessant refinement of the division of labour',[15] production had become more and more 'compartmentalised' or 'parcelised', so that the actual content of work had become trivial, absurd and meaningless. 'In the nineteenth century the concept of work retained a vestige of the notion of creativity', wrote Raoul Vaneigem. 'But Taylorism dealt the death-blow to a mentality which had been carefully fostered by archaic capitalism. It is useless to expect even a caricature of creativity from the conveyor-belt.'[16] The capitalist division of labour had also had the effect of creating a multitude of *specialists*, to the extent that it was now beyond anyone's ability to make sense of productive activity as a whole, or to comprehend the world as a unified totality.

However, the situationist critique of the society of the spectacle was far from limited solely to the sphere of production. The spectacle was also said to occupy all time spent outside of production, and it was to a critique of this sphere that the situationists devoted the greater part of their analyses. In order to understand this aspect of situationist theory, it is necessary to take a detour via another central concept in the situationists' ideas, again derived from Marxism: the contradiction between the material forces of production and the social relations of production.

In the context of situationist theory, it is perhaps more accurate and useful to see this 'contradiction' between the forces and relations of production in terms of a *contrast* between, on the one hand, the potential held out by the level of development of the material forces and, on the other hand, the actual reality imposed by the existing social relations; in other words, 'the appalling contrast between the possible constructions of life and its present poverty'.[17]

The situationists believed that during the course of the capitalist era the capitalist class had fulfilled the historic role of rapidly developing the forces of production, to the extent that previously utopian ideas about a communist organisation of society had now been provided with the material preconditions which would actually enable them to be turned into reality. The continuous expansion of scientific and technical capacities had brought about 'major break-throughs in the domination of nature',[18] so that the primary problem of the struggle for survival against nature had now undoubtedly been solved. The development of technology and automation also held out the prospect of the liberation of human energies from time-consuming and uncreative productive activity.

However, the projects made possible by the level of development of material forces remained locked within capitalism by the existing social relations. *Natural* alienation – the struggle for survival against nature – may have been overcome, but *social* alienation persisted, in the form of a hierarchical division between 'masters' and 'slaves'. This hierarchy had been a necessity at one stage in human history if the material preconditions for communism were to be created, but it had now outlived its usefulness. The existing social relations had become a *fetter*; not, it was emphasised, in the sense that henceforth capitalism would be 'doomed to automatically stagnate and become incapable of continuing its development', but in the sense that the existing social relations stood in the way of 'the grandiose *possible development* that could be based on the present economic infrastructure'.[19]

The situationists coined a new theory of 'immiseration' to express this contrast between present reality and the possibilities opened up by the era of capitalist development: *quantitative* poverty, in the sense of the material struggle for survival, had been more or less eradicated, but its elimination had been accompanied by a corresponding increase in a new *qualitative* poverty of everyday life. As Vaneigem put it: 'As poverty has been reduced in terms of mere material survival, it has become more profound in terms of our way of life';[20] or, more bluntly, 'Who wants a world in which the guarantee that we shall not die of starvation entails the risk of dying of boredom?'[21]

The situationists regarded this 'new poverty' as an inherent feature of what they referred to as 'superequipped' or 'overdeveloped' capitalism. Once the development of the capitalist mode of production had reached the point where the battle for survival against nature had been won and everyone's basic material needs had been supplied, what justification was there for the system's continued existence? And how was the system to remain in being? In the situationists' analysis, capitalism's survival now depended on its ability to make people buy and consume ever-increasing quantities of goods. 'Economic necessity' had been replaced by 'the necessity for boundless economic development'.[22] Vaneigem argued that 'the present economic system can only be rescued by turning man into a consumer, by identifying him with the largest possible number of consumable values', and he quoted a remark made by Eisenhower – 'To save the economy, we must buy, buy anything' – in support of his argument.[23]

Since, according to the situationists, everyone's basic material needs had already been satisfied, the increased consumption which capitalism sought depended on the successful fabrication, by means of advertising, news, culture, the mass media and other mechanisms of conditioning and suggestion, of an accelerating turnover of '*pseudo-needs*'. The survival of capitalism now depended on a dual collaboration from the working class; first, as always, in its role as producer, and second, but now much more vitally, in its role as consumer: 'alienated consumption becomes for the masses a duty supplementary to alienated production . . . as soon as the production of commodities reaches a surplus'. The worker is:

> suddenly redeemed from the total contempt which is clearly shown him by all varieties of organisation and supervision of production, [and] finds himself every day, outside of production and in the guise of a consumer, seemingly treated as an adult, with zealous politeness.[24]

As well as guaranteeing a never-ending supply of 'the consumer stimulus necessary for economic expansion',[25] the creation of pseudo-needs was also useful in ensuring the survival of capitalism as a social system. As the time spent in production was decreasing even under capitalism, the system fulfilled its need to control and pacify the working class in the time spent outside production by turning this increased leisure time itself into a commodity to be passively consumed. 'The ruling class', wrote Debord:

> has succeeded in using the leisure the revolutionary proletariat wrested from it by developing a vast industrial sector of leisure activities that is an incomparable instrument for stupefying the proletariat with by-products of mystifying ideology and bourgeois tastes.[26]

The consumption of pseudo-needs also served to increase passivity, separation and alienation: 'From the automobile to television, all *goods selected* by the spectacular system are also its weapons for a constant reinforcement of the conditions of isolation of "lonely crowds".'[27] In short, people had been increasingly freed from material poverty and the imperatives of production, but only to be increasingly trapped by qualitative poverty and the imperatives of consumption.

So much for the situationists' description and analysis of the society imposed by the existing social relations. Against this, they posed a vision of the sort of society which could be created on the basis of the existing material forces. Although the SI did describe the new non-market society in terms of some of its 'negative' accomplishments – the abolition of money, commodity production, wage labour, classes, private property, the state and so on – their chief emphasis was on some of the more positive features of this future communist society. If capitalist society was a world totally beyond the control of its creators, in which people's time was filled by mind-numbing toil and the pursuit of pseudo-needs manufactured by the system in order to perpetuate its own existence, the situationists' vision of communism was of a society in which each and every individual would actively participate in the conscious, deliberate and uninterrupted transformation and reconstruction of every aspect and each moment of life. Indeed, it was from this sort of vision that the situationists derived their name, since for them 'A moment of life concretely and deliberately constructed',[28] or several such moments 'federated', with 'the pleasure in them' brought out and 'their promise of life' released,[29] was precisely what they meant by 'a constructed *situation*'.

In the new society, pseudo-needs would be replaced by *real desires*, which could easily be realised through placing at the disposal of everyone's dreams and creativity the fantastic material potential which had been created under capitalism. The 'economy of profit' would give way to '*an economy of desires*, which could be formulated as: technological society plus the imagination of what could be done with it'.[30] 'Work in the ordinary sense' would be eliminated in favour of a 'new type of free activity' in which the distinction between work and play would disappear;[31] there would be 'the development of a materially equipped creative power beyond the traditional categories of work time and rest and recreation time'.[32]

The situationists identified the force which would overthrow the existing society as the 'new' or 'enlarged' 'proletariat'. However, this view had not been accepted within the SI without some conflict. At the fourth SI conference, in September 1960, delegates were asked to give their views on what forces in society the SI could count on. The declaration of the German section attacked 'the tendency . . . to count on the existence of a revolutionary proletariat', since they 'strongly doubt[ed] the revolutionary capacities of the workers against the bureaucratic institutions that have dominated their movement'. The German section suggested that 'the SI should prepare to realise its programme on its own by mobilising the avant-garde artists'. Guy Debord responded with 'a sharp critique of these positions', while Attila Kotányi reminded the German delegates that 'even if since 1945 they have apparently seen passive and satisfied workers in Germany . . . in other advanced capitalist countries "wildcat" strikes have multiplied . . . [also] they vastly underestimate the German workers'. In the end the debate was settled when the German delegates retracted their views, although one sequel to this episode was the exclusion of the German section from the SI in February 1962.[33]

The SI's faith in the revolutionary potential of the working class distinguished it from many contemporary political groups and individuals. It had become fashionable to deny the working class's revolutionary capacities, or even that one could any longer speak of the existence of such a class, and to argue instead that the new revolutionary forces in society would be composed of such groups as students, blacks, and the 'oppressed peoples' of the Third World. The situationists rejected any such notions. At the time of the 'Strasbourg Scandal' the SI declared that 'the pitiful *student milieu* is of no interest to us',[34] while on the subject of Third World movements it wrote that:

> apocalyptic fears or hopes regarding the movements of revolt in the colonised or semicolonised countries overlook this central fact: the revolutionary project must be realised in the industrially advanced countries.[35]
>
> The revolutionary movements of the Third World can succeed only on the basis of a lucid contribution to global revolution.[36]

Raoul Vaneigem ridiculed the idea that the working class had 'disappeared':

> Where on earth can it be? Spirited away? Gone underground? Or has it been put in a museum? *Sociologi disputant.* We hear from some quarters that in the advanced industrial countries the proletariat no longer exists, that it has disappeared forever under an avalanche of sound systems, colour TVs, waterbeds, two-car garages and swimming pools. Others denounce this as sleight of hand and indignantly point out a few remaining workers whose low wages and wretched conditions do undeniably evoke the nineteenth century . . . the hunt is on for the starving, for the last of the proletarians. The prize goes to the one who sells him his car and his blender, his bar and his home library; the one who teaches him to see himself in the leering hero of an advertisement that reassures him: 'You smile when you smoke Brand X'.[37]

The SI interpreted the events in France in May-June 1968 as irrefutable confirmation of their view that 'the supposed passivity and "bourgeoisification" of the proletariat' was 'the eternal refrain of all the cretins of the century'.[38] As René Viénet wrote:

> In reality, if the revolutionary crisis of May showed anything it was precisely . . . that the proletariat had *not* been integrated, and is the major revolutionary force in modern society. Pessimists and sociologists have to do their homework

> again, along with the mouthpieces of underdevelopment, Black Power and Dutschkeism [i.e. 'student power'].[39]

Because of their emphasis on time spent *outside* production, the situationists did not define the working class in terms of wage labour. For example, they wrote that the 1968 occupation movement had seen 'the sudden return of the proletariat as a historical class, a proletariat *enlarged* to include a *majority* of the wage labourers of modern society'.[40] In other words, even this 'enlarged proletariat' did not include *all* wage labourers. Instead, the situationists defined the working class more in terms of its existence outside the production process: as 'all people who have no possibility of altering the social space-time that society allots for their consumption' (in contrast to 'the rulers', who were defined as 'those who organise this space-time, or who at least have a significant margin of personal choice'),[41] or as including anyone who is not 'the master of one's own activity, of one's own life, in the slightest degree'.[42] The SI argued that this category was now 'tending to encompass almost everybody',[43] through 'the progressive disappearance of the peasantry and by the extension of the logic of factory labour to a large sector of "services" and intellectual professions'.[44]

From the early 1960s the SI tried to draw attention to the new forms of struggle in which the 'new' or 'enlarged' proletariat was beginning to engage, and the new demands to which these struggles gave voice. These struggles and their demands were interpreted as the portents of a renewed working-class assault on capitalism forseen by the SI, whose predictions in this respect appeared to be fulfilled in 1968. The SI was not interested in the 'classical' demands of the working class; in their accounts of the occupation movement in France in 1968, for example, they were at pains to point out that the workers were not on strike for higher wages. 'Traditional' demands for wage increases and better working conditions had in any case been superseded, in the SI's view, by capitalism's own development. What the SI looked for instead were 'the new focuses of revolt'[45] which challenged the very basis of the system as they had analysed it – revolts against the commodity, 'urbanism', ideology and the spectacle, signs of the will to live revolting against the passivity, isolation and sheer boredom of everyday life. Among the 'new resistances' to 'the world of the spectacle' to which the SI drew attention were: the smashing of store windows and neon signs – the 'most symbolic' points of the 'decor . . . of consumer society'; attacks on cars – 'a gesture of self-defence against the central object of consumer alienation'; the destruction of newspaper plant machinery and attacks on television news reporters – 'concrete reactions against the forces of conditioning';[46] the rejection of 'organised work and life', by the 'lumpenproletariat' for example;[47] and rioting, theft and looting – 'a revolt against the commodity' – by the blacks of the Watts district of Los Angeles in August 1965.[48] Wildcat strikes were seen as another type of proto-revolutionary action, since the situationists regarded trade unions as 'a mechanism for integrating workers into capitalist society'[49] and as 'guardians of capitalism in the factories'.[50]

Obviously, many of these actions were carried out with only a dim awareness, if any, that they represented such a fundamental challenge to capitalist society as the SI made out. However, the SI believed that 'all situationist ideas are nothing other than faithful developments of acts attempted constantly by thousands of people to try and prevent another day from being no more than twenty-four hours of wasted time'.[51] The role of the SI in relation to these struggles was therefore to 'illuminate and co-ordinate the gestures of refusal and the signs of creativity that are defining the new contours of the proletariat';[52] the SI was to 'tell the masses *what they are already doing*'.[53] Criticism of capitalism existed *implicitly* in the struggles of the working class, and *explicitly* in the theories of the SI; the task was now to bring these two elements together in order to make the revolutionary process a conscious one, since 'Historical consciousness is an essential condition of social revolution.'[54]

Just as theory and action would fuse in revolutionary practice, so too would the SI dissolve itself into the mass revolutionary movement; any modern revolutionary organisation, they wrote, 'must explicitly aim to dissolve itself as a separate organisation at its moment of victory'.[55] With such a view of the role of their own organisation, the SI obviously did not see the revolution in terms of the seizure of power by a party. Instead, the SI regarded *workers' councils* as the form and means through which the new society would be created, organised and run. By workers' councils the SI meant 'sovereign rank-and-file assemblies, in the enterprises and the neighbourhoods',[56] federated locally, nationally and internationally through recallable, mandated delegates controlled by the base assemblies. These would be 'unitary' organisations, concentrating and unifying all functions of deliberation and decision-making and execution regarding every aspect of life. The workers' councils would enable direct and total democracy to be realised; there would be no representation, no specialists, no separation or externalisation of powers, and no hierarchy.

STRENGTHS AND WEAKNESSES

Situationism shared three main strengths in common with the other currents which represent non-market socialism. First, the situationists recognised capitalism as a worldwide system embracing every existing nation-state: 'In spite of apparent variations and oppositions, a single social form dominates the world.'[57] Thus the situationists opposed *all* factions of the ruling class, in or out of power, arguing that 'In no case can [revolutionary criticism] applaud a belligerent *state* or support the bureaucracy of an exploiting state in formation.'[58] One of the most important consequences of this belief was the situationists' clear denial that countries such as Russia, China, Cuba and so on were 'communist' or in any other way worthy of working-class support: 'The domination of bureaucratic state-capitalism over the workers is the opposite of socialism . . . Socialism exists wherever the workers themselves directly manage the entire society; it therefore exists neither in Russia nor in China nor anywhere else.'[59]

Second, the situationists had a clear conception of what the establishment of a new non-market society would have to involve in terms of abolishing the essential characteristics of capitalism. In *The Revolution of Everyday Life*, Raoul Vaneigem outlined some of the immediate tasks of the communist revolution:

> the concrete transcendence of work, of the division of labour and of the antagonism between work and play . . . the concrete transcendence of exchange . . . [and] the concrete transcendence of the State and of every kind of alienating collectivity.[60]

From the body of situationist theory as a whole, the abolition of classes, commodity production and private property could be added to Vaneigem's list.

Third, the situationists believed that no other force in society could carry out the communist revolution apart from the working class; consequently, they attached great importance to class consciousness. As we have seen, the SI's self-conceived role was to 'awaken consciousness', since it believed that widespread class consciousness was one of the essential conditions of the workers' revolution. The 'insurrection' of 1968 was said to have failed precisely because it lacked this dimension:

> in the last analysis the revolutionary mass did not have the time for an exact and real consciousness of what it was doing. And it is this inadequate relation between theory and practice which remains the fundamental trait of proletarian revolutions which fail.[61]

In other words, the situationists believed that although the working class was capable of acting through objectively radical *forms*, it would be unable to effect any real changes in society unless such actions were also informed by a radical *consciousness*.

To move on to distinctive strengths of situationist theory, two of these stand out in particular. First, by concentrating on the 'qualitative' aspects of 'everyday life', the situationists were able to evoke, with great accuracy and in a frequently poetic way, many of the emotions felt about life within capitalism. Surely no wage- or salary-earner could fail to recognise something of the poverty of their own everyday life in Vaneigem's description of the 'twenty-four hour cycle' which fills life 'from adolescence to retirement':

> dragged out of sleep at six every morning, jolted about in suburban trains, deafened by the racket of machinery,

> bleached and steamed by meaningless sounds and gestures, spun dry by statistical controls, and tossed out at the end of the day into the entrance halls of railway stations, those cathedrals of departure for the hell of weekdays and the nugatory paradise of weekends.[62]

In arguing that, as much as from any other factor, the necessity and desire for a complete change in society would arise from the sheer soul-destroying boredom and exhaustion of such an existence, the situationists seemed to be stating something very obvious, yet something which had been overlooked or underplayed by other revolutionary currents.

A second distinctive strength of situationism lay in its positive descriptions of the new society, in contrast to other portrayals which have concentrated on its necessary but none the less essentially negative features (the abolition of this, that and the other). Through their tentative yet imaginative explorations of the uses to which the material forces developed under capitalism could be put, the situationists suggested a vision of socialism/communism in which the scope of human achievement would be constrained only by the limits of the human imagination. Undoubtedly, the immediate tasks of a communist society would be to ensure that for the first time in history every person had enough to eat, clothes to wear, and a roof over his or her head. But whereas this has been the limit of some conceptions of communism, the situationists took it as a mere starting-point. Why stop at 'the provision of shelter', the situationists argued, when in communism it would be possible to construct a society in which 'Everyone will live in his own personal "cathedral", so to speak'?[63] By unleashing the creative imagination in this way, and also by touching on the changes which could be brought about in areas as diverse as inter-personal relationships or the construction of the environment, the situationists performed the invaluable service of never ceasing to emphasise just how different from capitalism communism will be in *every* aspect.

Many of the situationists' theoretical preoccupations – especially their earlier writings on town planning, architecture, the environment and so on – can be understood by reference to social trends in post-war France, a society undergoing rapid 'modernisation'. From the start of the 1950s French society entered a period of rapid urbanisation, brought about through a combination of migration from the countryside to the towns (remember Guy Debord's reference to 'the progressive disappearance of the peasantry') and an upsurge in the birthrate after the end of the Second World War. This led to a chronic housing shortage and urban congestion; Debord observed that the main problem of town planning had become how to ensure 'the smooth circulation of a rapidly increasing quantity of motor vehicles'.[64] In Paris one of the proposed 'solutions' to the housing shortage involved a plan to make the city 'polycentric', by ringing it with five new suburban cities where people would be housed in tower blocks. Conceivably these were the 'most recent examples of city planning' which Raoul Vaneigem had in mind when he wrote of the 'labyrinths in which you are only allowed to lose yourself. No games. No meetings. No living. A desert of plate-glass. A grid of roads. High-rise flats',[65] or which he and Kotányi were describing when they referred to 'those bleak, brightly coloured kindergartens, the new dormitory cities'.[66] Workers had to travel great distances from these residential areas on the outskirts of the city to their places of work, which explains why the situationists included among the new focuses of working-class discontent the 'revolt against *commuting time*, which is such a burdensome addition to wage slavery time in modern cities'.[67]

The 'baby boom' of the post-war era also meant, obviously, that there were larger than ever numbers of young people in the population. Hence the references in situationist writings to 'youth rebellion', and the material for their idea that 'the teenager' was a 'social category invented for the needs of the commodity economy by sociologists and economists'.[68] There was also a vast expansion of the numbers in higher education, so that the situationists could write that 'The various faculties and schools that once supplied "general culture" to the ruling class . . . are being transformed into force-feeding factories for the accelerated rearing of lower and middle cadres.'[69]

The most noticeable feature of the post-war era in France was that from around 1950 onwards it was a period of sustained economic growth, fuelled by Marshall Aid and directed by the state through the Monnet Plans. Industrial production regained its highest pre-war level in 1951, and tripled over the next twenty years. The real purchasing power of the average French worker's wage rose by 170 per cent between 1950 and 1975, and overall consumption rose by 174 per cent during the same period. Personal expenditure on 'leisure activities' quadrupled in real terms between 1950 and 1977. This, of course, was the very stuff of the situationists' ideas about the consumption of leisure time, consumer durables, and so on. In 1956 French workers won the legal right to three weeks holiday per year, extended to four weeks in 1965. An increasing number of these holidays were spent abroad, which was perhaps the phenomenon that prompted Debord to describe tourism as 'human circulation considered as consumption . . . fundamentally nothing more than the leisure of going to see what has become banal'.[70]

The situationists were thus acute observers of the world around them. This was the source of many perceptive insights, but, paradoxically, it was also the source of their greatest weaknesses; they mistakenly projected the specific conditions of post-war France onto every other part of the contemporary world, and they mistook a temporary period of economic boom for a permanent state of affairs.

The situationists exaggerated the extent of working-class affluence in the capitalist heartlands even at the height of the period of economic growth. Yet even these exaggerations appear relatively insignificant when the terms in which the situationists described everyday life are compared with the reality of existence for millions of people in other vast areas of the world during the same period. In the underdeveloped countries – the 'Third World' – the primitive battle for survival against nature was nowhere near having been won. Far from dying of boredom under an avalanche of artificial pseudo-needs – 'sound systems, colour TVs, waterbeds, two-car garages and swimming pools' – the poor in these parts of the globe were, and still are, dying from a lack of real material needs – food, water, clothing, shelter and so on. Situationist theory – based on an exaggeration of tendencies in the advanced capitalist heartlands – did not appear to address this reality in any relevant way.

Now that the heartlands of the world capitalist system are themselves in the midst of an inexorably deepening crisis, many of the situationists' comments of twenty years ago appear absurdly shortsighted today: for example, Debord's claim that 'the constant intervention of the State has succeeded in compensating for the effects of tendencies toward crisis',[71] and his talk of 'the undisturbed development of modern capitalism',[72] or Vaneigem's comment that 'the economy cannot stop making us consume more and more'.[73] It need not be hindsight alone that makes the situationists look foolish; a basic tenet of Marxist economics is that periods of boom within capitalism can only be temporary, and that economic crisis is just as inherent a feature of the system. In this respect, it has been 'the vanity of those socialist calculations which thought they had established the exact periodicity of crises'[74] and 'those who cling to the classical calculation of the date of the next cyclical crisis of the economy'[75] who have survived the passage of time rather better than the situationists.

The return of the economic crisis obviously has profound implications for the situationists' views on the actual struggles of the working class. Anyone engaged in the 'hunt . . . for the starving', for those 'few remaining workers [with] low wages and wretched conditions' would not have to look far afield today (not that it would have been a fruitless search in Vaneigem's day). 'Traditional' or 'classical' demands dominate workers' struggles today, and the 'new demands' – which were no more than embryonic even in the situationists' own time – would now be difficult to detect. Where is the 'rejection of work' or the demand for its 'suppression' to be found in unemployed workers' demonstrations for 'the right to work'? Where can any demand for the 'abolition of wage labour' be detected in workers' struggles to fight redundancies and save jobs?

Naturally, this could be a cause of despair or despondency for any revolutionaries, not just the situationists. Of course it would be ideal if every time workers went on strike it was for the abolition of the wages system. But while this is not the situation in which revolutionaries presently find themselves, neither is it a reason for ignoring or abstaining from any struggle which starts out on the basis of ostensibly reformist demands (as latter-day situationists have tended to do). It is safe to say that the major issue confronting revolutionaries is how a working class preoccupied with reformist ends is going to transform itself into a revolutionary force; what is equally certain is that revolutionary consciousness will not drop from the skies one day like some *deus ex machina*. Communism will be brought about by a class – the working class – which exists and can be identified now, and revolutionary consciousness will emerge from this class's involvement in struggles which are every bit as concrete and visible.

Notes

1. 'Now, the SI', *Internationale Situationniste*, 9 (August 1964), in K. Knabb, *Situationist International Anthology* (Berkeley: Bureau of Public Secrets, 1981) p. 135.
2. Guy Debord, 'The Organisation Question for the SI', *Internationale Situationniste*, 12 (September 1969), in Knabb, 1981, p. 298.
3. 'The Bad Days Will End', *Internationale Situationniste*, 7 (April 1962), in Knabb, 1981, pp. 84–5.
4. 'The Beginning of an Era', *Internationale Situationniste*, 12 (September 1969), in Knabb, 1981, p. 249.
5. Quoted in Chris Gray, *The Incomplete Work of the Situationist International* (no place: Free Fall Publications, 1974) p. 86.
6. 'Our Goals and Methods in the Strasbourg Scandal', *Internationale Situationniste*, 11 (October 1967), in Knabb, 1981, p. 208.
7. René Viénet, *The Enragés and the Situationists in the Occupation Movement – France, May–June 1968* (York: Tiger Papers Publications, no date) p. 4.
8. Gray, 1974, p. 88.
9. Viénet, *The Enragés*, p. 19.
10. Gray, 1974, p. 165. For texts dealing with the period between the May–June events in France (1968) and the formal dissolution of the SI (1972), see Situationist International, *The Veritable Split in the International* (London: BM Chronos, 1985).
11. Raoul Vaneigem, 1972 Postscript to *The Revolution of Everyday Life* (no place: Left Bank Books and Rebel Press, 1983) p. 215.
12. For examples of situationist-inspired propaganda from France, Sweden, New Zealand, Italy, Belgium, England and the USA, see Steef Davidson, *The Penguin Book of Political Comics* (Harmondsworth: Penguin, 1982) pp. 56–85. Knabb, 1981, and Gray, 1974 both give some information about the influence of the Situationist International outside France and about post-1972 developments.
13. Guy Debord, *The Society of the Spectacle* (Detroit: Black and Red, 1977) thesis 26.

14. Ibid, theses 31 and 33 (emphases in the original).
15. Ibid, thesis 25.
16. Vaneigem, 1983, p. 38.
17. 'Instructions for Taking Up Arms', *Internationale Situationniste*, 6 (August 1961), in Knabb, 1981, p. 64.
18. 'The Sound and the Fury', *Internationale Situationniste*, 1 (June 1958), in Knabb, 1981, p. 41.
19. 'Ideologies, Classes and the Domination of Nature', *Internationale Situationniste*, 8 (January 1963), in Knabb, 1981, p. 104 (emphasis in the original).
20. Raoul Vaneigem, 'Basic Banalities' (part I), *Internationale Situationniste*, 7 (April 1962), in Knabb, 1981, p. 90.
21. Vaneigem, 1983, p. 8.
22. Debord, 1977, thesis 51.
23. Vaneigem, 1983, pp. 48 and 50.
24. Debord, 1977, theses 42–3.
25. 'Geopolitics of Hibernation', *Internationale Situationniste*, 7 (April 1962), in Knabb, 1981, p. 78.
26. Guy Debord, 'Report on the Construction of Situations and on the International Situationist Tendency's Conditions of Organisation and Action' (June 1957), in Knabb, 1981, p. 24.
27. Debord, 1977, thesis 28 (emphasis in the original).
28. 'Definitions', *Internationale Situationniste*, 1 (June 1958), in Knabb, 1981, p. 45.
29. Vaneigem, 1983, p. 68.
30. 'The Bad Days Will End', in Knabb, 1981, p. 87 (emphasis in the original).
31. 'Ideologies, Classes and the Domination of Nature', in Knabb, 1981, p. 102.
32. 'Instructions for Taking Up Arms', in Knabb, 1981, p. 64.
33. 'The Fourth SI Conference in London', *Internationale Situationniste*, 5 (December 1960), in Knabb, 1981, p. 62.
34. 'Our Goals and Methods in the Strasbourg Scandal', in Knabb, 1981, p. 207 (emphasis in the original).
35. 'The Bad Days Will End', in Knabb, 1981, p. 85.
36. 'Address to Revolutionaries of Algeria and of All Countries', *Internationale Situationniste*, 10 (March 1966), in Knabb, 1981, p.150.
37. Vaneigem, 1983, pp. 48–9.
38. *On the Poverty of Student Life*, in Knabb, 1981, p. 328.
39. Viénet, *The Enragés*, p. 17.
40. 'The Beginning of an Era', in Knabb, 1981, p. 225 (emphasis added).
41. 'Ideologies, Classes and the Domination of Nature', in Knabb, 1981, p. 108.
42. 'The Decline and Fall of the Spectacle-Commodity Economy', *Internationale Situationniste*, 10 (March 1966), in Knabb, 1981, p. 156.
43. 'The Bad Days Will End', in Knabb, 1981, p. 85.
44. Debord, 1977, thesis 114.
45. 'The Beginning of an Era', in Knabb, 1981, p. 227.
46. 'The Bad Days Will End', in Knabb, 1981, p. 83.

47. Raoul Vaneigem, 'Basic Banalities' (part II), *Internationale Situationniste*, 8 (January 1963), in Knabb, 1981, pp. 126–7.
48. 'The Decline and Fall of the Spectacle-Commodity Economy', in Knabb, 1981, pp. 153-60.
49. Council for the Continuation of Occupations (CMDO), 'For the Power of the Workers' Councils' (22 May 1968), in Knabb, 1981, p. 349.
50. Viénet, *The Enragés*, p. 13.
51. Vaneigem, 'Basic Banalities' (part II), in Knabb, 1981, p. 123.
52. 'Questionnaire', *Internationale Situationniste*, 9 (August 1964), in Knabb, 1981, p. 139.
53. 'The Class Struggles in Algeria', *Internationale Situationniste*, 10 (March 1966), in Knabb, 1981, p. 166 (emphasis in the original).
54. Viénet, *The Enragés*, p. 17.
55. 'Minimum Definition of Revolutionary Organisations', *Internationale Situationniste*, 11 (October 1967), in Knabb, 1981, p. 223.
56. 'The Beginning of an Era', in Knabb, 1981, p. 253.
57. *On the Poverty of Student Life*, in Knabb, 1981, p. 332.
58. 'Two Local Wars', *Internationale Situationniste*, 11 (October 1967), in Knabb, 1981, p. 196.
59. 'Address to Revolutionaries of Algeria and of All Countries', in Knabb, 1981, p. 149.
60. Vaneigem, 1983, p. 211.
61. Viénet, *The Enragés*, p. 17.
62. Vaneigem, 1983, p. 37.
63. Ivan Chtcheglov, 'Formulary for a New Urbanism' (October 1953), in Knabb, 1981, p. 3.
64. Guy Debord, 'Introduction to a Critique of Urban Geography' (September 1955), in Knabb, 1981, p. 5.
65. Vaneigem, 1983, p. 188.
66. Attila Kotányi and Raoul Vaneigem, 'Elementary Programme of the Bureau of Unitary Urbanism', *Internationale Situationniste*, 6 (August 1961), in Knabb, 1981, p. 66.
67. 'The Bad Days Will End', in Knabb, 1981, p. 83 (emphasis in the original).
68. Viénet, *The Enragés*, p. 15.
69. *On the Poverty of Student Life*, in Knabb, 1981, p. 322.
70. Debord, 1977, thesis 168.
71. Ibid, thesis 82.
72, Ibid, thesis 65.
73. Vaneigem, 1983, p. 14.
74. Debord, 1977, thesis 82.
75. Guy Debord, 'Perspectives for Conscious Alterations in Everyday Life', *Internationale Situationniste*, 6 (August 1961), in Knabb, 1981, p. 73.

Postscript

In writing this book, we have been motivated strongly by an urgent desire to convince our readers of non-market socialism's contemporary relevance as the only solution to the problems confronting the wage-working class. We hope that readers will be sufficiently interested in our arguments to want to discover more about non-market socialism. For the benefit of such readers, we are providing information about organisations which are currently active in propagating the ideas discussed in this book.

For two main reasons, we have not attempted to compile a comprehensive directory of non-market socialist organisations and publications. First, such a directory would require constant revision and up-dating. The same conditions of life under capitalism which continually evoke a non-market socialist response from within the wage-earning class also contain powerful forces which militate against sustained opposition to capitalism. Thus non-market socialist groups come and go; organisations such as the Socialist Party of Great Britain, with a record of over eighty years' unbroken commitment to non-market socialism, are the exception rather than the rule. The fleeting existence of many non-market socialist groups is, for us, a matter for regret; at the same time, however, the unfailing emergence of new groups which take their place is confirmation of our view that non-market socialism is a recurrent response to capitalism on the part of the working class.

Our second reason for refraining from any attempt to compile a comprehensive directory is that while those who become non-market socialists sometimes derive their ideas from one or more of the currents analysed in this book, on other occasions organised expressions of non-market socialism emerge as a spontaneous assertion of the non-market socialist alternative to capitalism, with little or no reference to previous traditions or to other non-market socialist groups. Thus although the authors of this book have had many years' involvement in, and contact with, revolutionary groups in many parts of the world, we can be quite confident that throughout the world there are still non-market socialist groups that we have never heard of, and that have never heard of us. It is the very vitality of non-market socialism which makes it impossible to keep track of its numerous manifestations, and which, again, confirms our view of its irrepressibility as a persistent response to the existing worldwide organisation of society.

In addition to information about existing political organisations, we shall also suggest various books and pamphlets which present non-market socialist ideas. This Postscript can therefore be read in conjunction with the Select Bibliography.

ANARCHO-COMMUNISM

In Chapter 3, Alain Pengam argues that after the 1920s the critical force that anarcho-communism had represented largely left the anarchist movement, but reappeared with certain communist currents that emerged in the 1970s. Besides the pamphlet which Pengam mentions – *Un Monde sans argent: le communisme* (discussed in Chapter 6) – one could also cite in this context the following pamphlets:

Ratgeb, *De la grève sauvage à l'autogestion généralisée* (Paris: Union générale d'éditions, 1974)
L'Insécurité Sociale, *Communisme: éléments de réflexion (1)* (Paris: L'Insécurité Sociale (Série II) No. 2, 1984)

An English translation of *De la grève sauvage à l'autogestion généralisée*, titled *Contributions to the Revolutionary Struggle*, has been published by Bratach Dubh (London: 1981). It advocates a society in which 'obligatory work will be replaced by a collective creativity regulated by the wishes of each individual, and by the free distribution of the goods necessary for our everyday needs'. *Communisme: éléments de réflexion* argues that the establishment of communism necessarily involves the disappearance of all property, states and money. This pamphlet may be obtained from L'Insécurité Sociale, BP 243, 75564 Paris Cedex 12, France.

The authors of these texts do not consciously situate themselves within the anarcho-communist tradition ('Ratgeb' is a pseudonym used by Raoul Vaneigem, some of whose writings are discussed in Chapter 7, on situationism; L'Insécurité Sociale emerged from the group Pour Une Intervention Communiste, which was in origin a council communist group). However, not all non-market socialist groups can be slotted easily into one of the five currents discussed in this book; with the emergence of new groups which tend to supersede old divisions by deriving their ideas from several sources, distinctions between some of the currents are becoming less meaningful.

IMPOSSIBILISM

In Chapter 4, Stephen Coleman discusses the Socialist Party of Great Britain (SPGB). The SPGB and its 'companion parties', may be contacted at the following addresses:
Socialist Party of Great Britain: 52 Clapham High Street, London SW4 7UN, GB.
World Socialist Party of Australia: PO Box 1440M, Melbourne, Victoria 3001, Australia.
Bund Demokratischer Sozialisten: Gussriegelstrasse 50, A-1100, Vienna, Austria.
Socialist Party of Canada: PO Box 4280 Station A, Victoria BC V8X 3X8 or CP 244, Pointe-aux-Trembles, Quebec HIB 5K3, Canada.
World Socialist Party (Ireland): 41 Donegall Street, Belfast, GB.
Socialist Party of New Zealand: PO Box 1929, Auckland NI, New Zealand.
World Socialist Party of the United States: PO Box 405, Boston, MA 02272, USA.
Varldssocialistika Gruppen: c/o Dag Nillson, Ymergatan 13c, S-753 25 Uppsala, Sweden.
French journal: *Socialisme Mondiale*, BP 26, 6700 Arlon, Belgium.

Two books which argue the case for impossibilism are: Samuel Leight, *World Without Wages* (Tucson: WWW Publishers, 1982) and, by the same author, *The Futility of Reformism* (Tucson: WWW Publishers, 1984). These are available from the SPGB or direct from WWW Publishers, PO Box 42224, Tucson, Arizona 85733, USA.

In Chapter 4, Coleman also refers to the Socialist Labour Party (SLP), which publishes a fortnightly newspaper called *The People*. The SLP's address is: PO Box 50218, Palo Alto, CA 94303, USA. There are several other groups in the USA which although organisationally separate from the SLP express basically the same ideas. A regular *Discussion Bulletin* is published as a forum for debate between these groups. The *Discussion Bulletin* can be obtained from PO Box 1564, Grand Rapids, MI 49501, USA.

COUNCIL COMMUNISM

In Chapter 5, Mark Shipway relies heavily on Anton Pannekoek's writings in order to explain council communist theories. The organisations with which Pannekoek was associated have long since vanished, and it is doubtful whether any 'orthodox' council communist groups exist today. However, aspects of the theoretical legacy of council communism survive in groups such as:

Communist Bulletin Group: Box CBG, Boomtown Books, 167 King Street, Aberdeen, GB.
International Communist Current. The ICC has 'sections' in Belgium, France, Great Britain, Italy, Netherlands, Spain, Sweden, USA, Venezuela and West Germany. Their addresses can be found in all ICC publications, or by writing to the British section – World Revolution – at BM Box 869, London WC1N 3XX, GB.
Wildcat: Box 1, Raven Press, 75 Piccadilly, Manchester M1 2BU, GB.

Anton Pannekoek's book, *Workers' Councils*, was republished in 1984 by Echanges et Mouvement (address: BM Box 91, London WC1N 3XX, GB). A bulletin called *Echanges*, available from the same address, is a useful source of information about publications of council communist and other non-market socialist groups.

One of the most productive authors in the council communist tradition was Paul Mattick (1904–81). In addition to *Anti-Bolshevik Communism* (see Select Bibliography), Mattick also wrote the following books:
Marx and Keynes: Limits of the Mixed Economy (London: Merlin, 1971)
Critique of Marcuse: One-Dimensional Man in Class Society (London: Merlin, 1972)
Economics, Politics, and the Age of Inflation (London: Merlin, 1980)
Economic Crisis and Crisis Theory (London: Merlin, 1981)
Marxism – Last Refuge of the Bourgeoisie? (London: Merlin, 1983)

BORDIGISM

In Chapter 6, Adam Buick mentions the International Communist Party (ICP). The ICP is one of several Bordigist groups currently in existence, but since it was the group with which Amadeo Bordiga was associated until his death in 1970, it is generally regarded as the 'official' or 'orthodox' representative of Bordigism.

In an article on 'The Myth of "Socialist Planning" in Russia' (*Communist Program*, 4, April 1978) the ICP argues that:

> Socialism therefore has no use for the market categories which reign as master over the Russian economy. It does not know *value* since there are no *private* products and thus no *exchange* between private producers, implying that the producers have no need to know the relative values of their products. It thus knows neither the market nor *commodities*, and still less the particular commodity *money*. It knows neither selling nor buying and thus neither the selling nor buying of the commodity *labour-power* or *wage-labour* which, for the Marxist, is abolished during the first phase of communist society, or socialism.

The ICP has published the journals *Programme Communiste* and *Le Prolétaire* in French, and the journal *Il Programma Comunista* in Italian. Its fundamental texts are also available in a variety of other languages, such as English, German, Spanish and Portuguese. The International Communist Party's address is c/o Valentini, 7 avenue de la Forêt Noire, 67000 Strasbourg, France.

SITUATIONISM

In Chapter 7, Mark Shipway quotes extensively from the *Situationist International Anthology* published by the Bureau of Public Secrets (see Select Bibliography). The Bureau of Public Secrets is also the author and publisher of several other pamphlets and texts which can be located within the situationist tradition. These may be obtained from the Bureau's address: PO Box 1044, Berkeley, California 94701, USA.

Two recent examples of situationist propaganda are:

Like a Summer with a Thousand July's (*sic*) (London: BM Blob, 1982)
Miner Conflicts – Major Contradictions (London: BM Combustion, 1984)

Like a Summer with a Thousand July's – an analysis of the riots in Britain in 1981 – may be obtained from BM Blob, London WC1N 3XX, GB. A French translation, with the same title, was published in 1985 by L'Eveil Internationaliste, BP 221, 44604 Saint-Nazaire Cedex, France. *Miner Conflicts – Major Contradictions* – a critique of the 'commodity-spectacle' which takes as its starting-point an analysis of the miners' strike in Britain in 1984–5 – is available from BM Combustion, London WC1N 3XX, GB.

Select Bibliography

Les Amis de 4 Millions de Jeunes Travailleurs, *Un Monde sans argent: le communisme* (Paris: Les Amis de 4 Millions de Jeunes Travailleurs, 1975).

Arnot, R. Page, *William Morris: the Man and the Myth* (London: Lawrence & Wishart, 1964).

Authier, Denis, and Barrot, Jean, *La Gauche communiste en Allemagne (1918–1921)* (Paris: Payot, 1976).

Avrich, Paul, *The Russian Anarchists* (Princeton: University Press, 1967).

Bahro, Rudolph, *The Alternative in Eastern Europe* (London: New Left Books, 1978).

Baldwin, Roger N., *Kropotkin's Revolutionary Pamphlets* (New York: Dover, 1970).

Barrot, Jean, and Martin, François, *Eclipse and Re-emergence of the Communist Movement* (Detroit: Black and Red, 1974).

Berkman, Alexander, *ABC of Anarchism* (London: Freedom Press, 1977).

——, *The Russian Tragedy* (Sanday: Cienfuegos, 1976).

——, *What Is Communist Anarchism?* (New York: Vanguard, 1929).

Bordiga, Amadeo, 'Dictature prolétarienne et parti de classe', in *Textes fondamentaux de la gauche communiste* in *La Révolution Communiste*, 3 (Brussels: 1984).

——, *Russie et révolution dans la théorie marxiste* (Paris: Spartacus, 1978).

——, *Socialisme prolétarien contre socialisme petit-bourgeois* (Paris: International Communist Party, 1980).

——, *Structure économique et sociale de la Russie d'aujourd'hui* (Paris: Editions de l'Oubli, 1975).

The Bourgeois Role of Bolshevism (Glasgow: Glasgow People's Press, no date).

Brémond, Raoul, *La Communauté* (Paris: Editions de l'Oubli, 1975).

Bricianer, Serge, *Pannekoek and the Workers' Councils* (Saint Louis: Telos, 1978).

Britel, Gaston, *La Foire aux ânes ou de l'Abolition du salariat* (no place: Editions de la Moisson Nouvelle, 1951).

Buick, Adam, 'William Morris and Incomplete Communism: a Critique of Paul Meier's Thesis', *Journal of the William Morris Society*, III (summer 1976).

Buick, Adam, and Crump, John, *State Capitalism: the Wages System under New Management* (London: Macmillan, 1986).

Cafiero, C., *Communisme et Anarchisme* (Paris: Groupe Eugène Varlin de la Fédération anarchiste, 1982).

Camatte, Jacques, *Bordiga et la passion du communisme: Textes essentiels de Bordiga et repères biographiques* (Paris: Spartacus, 1974).

——, *Capital et Gemeinwesen* (Paris: Spartacus, 1976).

Coleman, Stephen, 'The Origin and Meaning of the Political Theory of Impossibilism' (unpublished Ph.D. thesis, University of London, 1984).

——, 'What Can We Learn From William Morris?' *Journal of the William Morris Society*, VI (summer 1985).

Communist Workers' Party of Germany (KAPD), 'Theses on the Party', *Revolutionary Perspectives*, 2 (no date).
Craver, Earlene, 'The Rediscovery of Amadeo Bordiga', *Survey*, XX (spring/summer 1974).
Crump, John, *A Contribution to the Critique of Marx* (London: Social Revolution/Solidarity, 1975).
Davidson, Steef, *The Penguin Book of Political Comics* (Harmondsworth: Penguin, 1982).
De Clementi, Andreina, *Amadeo Bordiga* (Turin: Einaudi, 1971).
Debord, Guy, *The Society of the Spectacle* (Detroit: Black and Red, 1977).
Déjacque, Joseph, *A bas les chefs!* (Paris: Champ Libre, 1970).
Engels, Frederick, *Anti-Dühring* (Peking: Foreign Languages Press, 1976).
Faure, Sebastien, *Mon Communisme* (Paris: Editions de 'La Fraternelle', 1921).
Fernbach, David, *Karl Marx: the Revolutions of 1848 – Political Writings* (Harmondsworth: Penguin, 1973).
Galleani, Luigi, *The End of Anarchism?* (Sanday: Cienfuegos, 1982).
Gorter, Herman, *The Communist Workers' International* (London: 1977).
——, 'Manifesto of the Fourth Communist International', in *Workers' Dreadnought*, 8 October–10 December 1921.
——, 'Reply to Lenin', in *Workers' Dreadnought*, 12 March–11 June 1921.
——, *The World Revolution* (Glasgow: Socialist Information and Research Bureau (Scotland), 1920).
Gray, Chris, *The Incomplete Work of the Situationist International* (no place: Free Fall Publications, 1974).
Group of International Communists of Holland (GIC), 'Temps de travail social moyen: base d'une production et d'une répartition communiste'. Supplement to *Informations Correspondances Ouvrières*, 101 (1971).
——, *Theses on Bolshevism*: see *The Bourgeois Role of Bolshevism*.
Guillaume, James, *Idées sur l'organisation sociale* (Paris: Volonté Anarchiste no. 8 – Edition du groupe Fresnes-Antony de la Fédération anarchiste, 1979).
Hyndman, H. M., *Further Reminiscences* (London: Macmillan, 1912).
International Communist Current (ICC), *La Gauche communiste d'Italie* (Brussels: International Communist Current, 1983).
International Communist Party (ICP), *Bilan d'une révolution* (Paris: International Communist Party, 1967–8).
Internationale Situationniste (Paris: 1958–69).
Jackson, T. A., *Solo Trumpet* (London: Lawrence & Wishart, 1953).
Knabb, Ken, *Situationist International Anthology* (Berkeley: Bureau of Public Secrets, 1981).
Kraus, Karl, *Sprüche und Widersprüche* (Vienna/Leipzig: 1924).
Kropotkine, Pierre, *L'Anarchie, sa philosophie, son idéal* (Paris: Publico, 1981).
Kropotkin, Peter, *The Conquest of Bread* (New York: University Press, 1972).
Kropotkine, Pierre, *Fatalité de la révolution* (Toulouse: Editions CNT, 1975).
Kropotkin, Peter, *Fields, Factories and Workshops* (New York: Greenwood, 1968).
Kropotkine, Pierre Alekseievitch, *Paroles d'un révolté* (Paris: Flammarion, 1978).
Kropotkine, Pierre, *Le Salariat* (1911), reissued by Le 'Combat Syndicaliste' (Paris: 1973).

Lenin, V. I., *Collected Works* (Moscow: Foreign Languages Publishing House, 1960–70).
Luxemburg, Rosa, *Leninism or Marxism* (Glasgow: Anti-Parliamentary Communist Federation, 1935).
——, *The Mass Strike, the Political Party and the Trade Unions* (London: Merlin, no date).
Magon, R. F., *Land and Liberty: Anarchist Influences in the Mexican Revolution* (Sanday: Cienfuegos, 1977).
Maîtron, J., *Histoire du mouvement anarchiste en France* (Paris: Maspero, 1978).
Malatesta, Errico, *Articles politiques* (Paris: Union générale d'éditions 10/18, 1979).
——, *Ecrits choisis* (Annecy: Groupe 1er Mai, 1981).
Mandel, Ernest, *Marxist Economic Theory* (London: Merlin, 1968).
Mannheim, Karl, *Ideology and Utopia* (London: Routledge, 1936).
Man's Dreams Are Coming True (Moscow: Progress, 1966).
Marx, Karl, *Capital* (Chicago: Charles H. Kerr, 1919).
Marx, Karl, and Engels, Frederick, *Collected Works* (London: Lawrence & Wishart, 1975–).
Marx, Karl, and Engels, Friedrich, *Ex libris Karl Marx und Friedrich Engels. Schicksal und Verzeichnis einer Bibliothek* (Berlin: Dietz Verlag, 1967).
Marx, Karl, and Engels, Frederick, *Selected Works* (Moscow: Progress, 1969–70).
Mattick, Paul, *Anti-Bolshevik Communism* (London: Merlin, 1978).
Miller, Martin A., *Kropotkin* (Chicago: University Press, 1976).
Morris, William, *Collected Works* (London: Longman, 1910–15).
——, *News From Nowhere* (London: Routledge, 1970).
——, *True and False Society* (Socialist League, 1888).
Morton, A. L., *Political Writings of William Morris* (London: Lawrence & Wishart, 1973).
Nettlau, Max, *Histoire de l'anarchie, Les dossiers de l'histoire* (Paris: Editions de l'Université et de l'Enseignement moderne, 1983).
Noland, Aaron, *The Founding of the French Socialist Party, 1893–1905* (New York: Fertig, 1970).
Ōsugi, Sakae, 'Rōnō Roshia no Shin Rōdō Undō', in *Ōsugi Sakae Zenshū*, vol. II (Tokyo: 1963).
Panicker, M. J., *20th Century World Socialist or Communist Manifesto* (London: Panicker, 1951).
Pannekoek, Anton, *Lenin As Philosopher* (London: Merlin, 1975).
——, *Workers' Councils* (Cambridge, Mass.: Root and Branch, 1970).
Pataud, Emile, and Pouget, Emile, *Syndicalism and the Co-operative Commonwealth. How We Shall Bring About the Revolution* (Oxford: New International, 1913).
Pelosse, V., 'J. Déjacque et la création du néologisme "libertaire" (1857)', *Etudes de Marxologie*, VI (December 1972).
Philoren, *Money Must Go* (London: J. Phillips, 1943).
Rancière, J., and Faure, A., *La Parole ouvrière, 1830–1851* (Paris: Union générale, 1976).
Reclus, Elisée, *L'Homme et la terre* (Paris: Maspero, 1982).
Rubel, Maximilien, 'Marx théoricien de l'anarchisme', in *Les Cahiers du Vent du Ch'min*, 5 (Saint-Denis: 1983).

Rubel, Maximilien, and Manale, Margaret, *Marx Without Myth* (Oxford: Blackwell, 1975).
Rühle, Otto, *From the Bourgeois to the Proletarian Revolution* (London and Glasgow: Socialist Reproduction/Revolutionary Perspectives, 1974).
——, *Karl Marx, His Life and Work* (London: George Allen & Unwin, 1929).
Situationist International, *The Veritable Split in the International* (London: BM Chronos, 1985).
Skirda, Alexandre, *Nestor Makhno, le Cosaque de l'Anarchie* (Paris: Skirda, 1982).
Smart, D. A., *Pannekoek and Gorter's Marxism* (London: Pluto, 1978).
Socialist Labor Party (SLP), *Socialism: Questions Most Frequently Asked and Their Answers* (New York: Socialist Labor Party, 1975).
Socialist Party of Australia, *Socialism or Chaos* (Melbourne/Sydney: Socialist Party of Australia, no date).
Socialist Party of Canada, *Lenin Distorts Marx* (Victoria: Socialist Party of Canada, 1979).
Socialist Party of Great Britain (SPGB), *Beveridge Re-Organises Poverty* (London: Socialist Party of Great Britain, 1943).
——, *The Case for Socialism* (London: Socialist Party of Great Britain, 1962).
——, *Family Allowances: a Socialist Analysis* (London: Socialist Party of Great Britain, 1943).
——, *Nationalisation or Socialism?* (London: Socialist Party of Great Britain, 1945).
——, *Questions of the Day* (London: Socialist Party of Great Britain, 1978).
——, *The Socialist Party and War* (London: Socialist Party of Great Britain, 1970).
——, *The Socialist Party – Its Principles and Policy* (London: Socialist Party of Great Britain, 1934).
——, *The Socialist Party of Great Britain and Historical Materialism* (London: Socialist Party of Great Britain, 1975).
——, *Socialist Principles Explained* (London: Socialist Party of Great Britain, 1975).
Socialist Standard (London, 1904–).
Sorel, Georges, 'L'Ethique du socialisme', *Revue de Métaphysique et du Morale*, VII (May 1899).
——, *Matériaux pour une théorie du prolétariat* (Paris: Marcel Rivière, 1921).
——, 'Morale et socialisme', *Le Mouvement Social*, I (March 1899).
Thompson, E. P., *The Making of the English Working Class* (London: Victor Gollancz, 1963).
——, *The Poverty of Theory* (London: Merlin, 1978).
——, *William Morris: Romantic to Revolutionary* (London: Merlin, 1977).
Tsuzuki, Chūshichi, 'The Impossibilist Revolt in Britain', *International Review of Social History*, I (1956).
Vaneigem, Raoul, *The Revolution of Everyday Life* (no place: Left Bank Books and Rebel Press, 1983).
——, *Traité de savoir-vivre à l'usage des jeunes générations:* see Vaneigem, *The Revolution of Everyday Life*.

Viénet, René, *The Enragés and the Situationists in the Occupation Movement – France, May–June 1968* (York: Tiger Papers Publications, no date).
Woodcock, G., and Avakumovič, I., *The Anarchist Prince* (London: Boardman, 1950).
Workers' Dreadnought (London: 1917–24).

Index